D1615824

ISLANDS OF IRELAND

Islands of the British Isles

ISLANDS OF IRELAND
ISLANDS OF SCOTLAND
ISLANDS OF ENGLAND AND WALES

ISLANDS OF IRELAND

Donald McCormick

 Osprey

First published in 1974 by
Osprey Publishing Ltd, P.O. Box 25,
707 Oxford Road, Reading, Berkshire

© Copyright 1974 Donald McCormick
All rights reserved

Filmset in Monophoto Plantin by
BAS Printers Limited, Wallop, Hampshire
ISBN 0 85045 168 X

INTRODUCTION

Scattered around the Irish coastline, mainly on the western side, is a great profusion of islands and islets of all shapes and sizes. If one counted every little speck of land that peeped out of the water, the total would exceed a thousand, but it must be confessed that the vast majority would be rocks or sandbanks.

Purists reject the inclusion as islands of 'all mere rocks which are the resort of wild fowl', but to keep rigidly to this axiom would rule out such fascinating rock islands as Carrick-a-Rede, with its swinging bridge, and the legendary Diarmuid and Grainne's Island. I have preferred to give the benefit of the doubt to certain islands which the purists would omit from a book such as this, and to ponder on those words of R. M. Lockley: 'There is something about a small island that satisfies the heart of man. "Ah, if only that little island were mine. What fun I could have with it!" we say. And we plan what we could do with a little kingdom of our own set in the silver sea.'

For the purpose of this book I have omitted all islands in inland loughs and the upper reaches of rivers. I have, however, included such islands in river estuaries as the various clusters of islets in the River Shannon estuary and the many delightful islands in Strangford Lough in Northern Ireland, which has a narrow neck leading into the sea.

Islands linked to the mainland by a causeway at low water, yet totally isolated at high water, have been included, but those which are joined to the mainland by road or bridge have, generally speaking, been excluded. However, I have not always kept strictly to such rules as there seemed to be some special cases where they should be waived. For example I have made exceptions for the islands of Gorumna, Lettermore, and Lettermullen, which are all linked together by roads and causeways. Here I felt that the test was the island spirit and atmosphere had not been destroyed by roads and causeways. Similarly it seemed foolish, if logical, to omit Ireland's largest island, Achill, just because it was joined to the mainland by a bridge. In all other respects Achill is essentially an island-lover's island.

Some of the smallest islands have been given more space than their sizes would seem to justify. One such is Garinish in Bantry Bay, which is a superb example of how a bare waste of only 37 acres has been turned into gardens of exotic and sub-tropical beauty. Another is Dorinish in the north-west, where an even less promising waste of 25 acres has in recent years been made the site for an experiment in community life.

By using the maps it will be feasible to plan a series of excursions to take in a group of islands at a time. It should be stressed that there are very many groups of literally scores of small islands: those in Roaringwater Bay alone would take several days to explore properly, and one could easily spend two weeks in the Aran Islands before exhausting all the sight-seeing possibilities.

I have tried to give the kind of information a wide range of island-lovers will desire: how to get there;

the problems of finding a landing-place and how you can walk out to some islands when the tide is out; details of accommodation where this is available; climate; and recreational facilities. I have also tried to indicate the scope for people with special interests: bird-watchers (Saltee off Wexford is an absolute 'must' for ornithologists, and Bristol University has organised a bird-watching station at Cape Clear Island); archaeologists (probably no other groups of islands in the world offer so much for them); botanists; historians; climbers; fishermen; yachtsmen; geologists; people in quest of solitude (the Blaskets are a paradise for them); youth in search of adventure and sailing courses (the Glenans Sailing Centre for boys and girls operates around Bere Island); those whose tastes are for *ceilidh* concerts in remote Gaelic outposts (Inishmore and elsewhere); marine biologists; golfers; animal lovers; the ordinary tourist who wants something different; hikers; honeymooners and romantics of all kinds.

Most of the islands have some legend woven around them or their names, and the superstitions attaching to them are so far-fetched that their repetition may suggest that the author is singularly credulous. I make no apology for including them: in many instances the legend seems to justify the very existence of the island. Most of the legends are rooted deep in Gaelic folk-lore.

Some of the uninhabited islands have been forgotten long since even by the most erudite mainlanders, and there is little to say about them except for their situation and size. I have nevertheless included a few such, with such sparse details, in the hope that some will be tempted to explore them. Such insignificant islands might one day emulate Garinish, if someone is possessed of Elizabeth Barrett Browning's longing:

> My dream is of an island-place
> Which distant seas keep lonely,
> A little island on whose face
> The stars are watchers only.

Many islands are named after saints – several after saints whose claims to canonisation are doubtful, and in some cases whose very existence is mythical. But they do bear witness to the fact that in the Dark Ages it was the tiny, remote islands off these coasts which alone bravely and nobly maintained traditions of Christianity and scholarship. Indeed the seat of learning that Enda set up in the Aran Islands was virtually the only 'university' in the Ireland of its time, and attracted 3,000 students from all parts of Europe.

Irish islands have been the birthplaces of some of the most outstanding literature of the country. The bleak outposts of the Blaskets produced a group of local writers from Maurice O'Sullivan and Tomas O'Crohan to Peig Sayers, all of whose works are still published. You will also find the literature of the islands in the short stories of Liam O'Flaherty, Synge, and Yeats, in *Some Irish Yesterdays* by that remarkable pair, Somerville and Ross, and in many of the Irish folk songs.

A book such as this requires constant revision, for whereas the mainland remains much the same, the tiniest islands have a habit of disappearing, due to erosion or changes in tidal or river currents, and occasionally there is that rarity, a new island rising out of the sea. Two other problems also confront the author: the size of an island, and its population. In some cases I have been faced with two widely differing

viii

sets of official figures for the size of an island, depending on whether the estimate was made at high tide or low. Similarly it has not always been easy to get up-to-date figures for population, especially as in many cases census figures have not covered all the very small islands. Sometimes, too, an island listed as uninhabited has seasonal residents and the figures given in (say) July may well differ from those in December (see the Blaskets). The figures given are for 1961 unless otherwise stated.

In concluding I should like to acknowledge the help I received in compiling this work and to express my gratitude to the Royal Geographical Society; the Regional Office of the National Trust in Northern Ireland; the Irish Tourist Office, especially for the enthusiastic help and advice given by Mr Fiach O Broin, of Dublin; and countless private owners of islands, too numerous to mention individually.

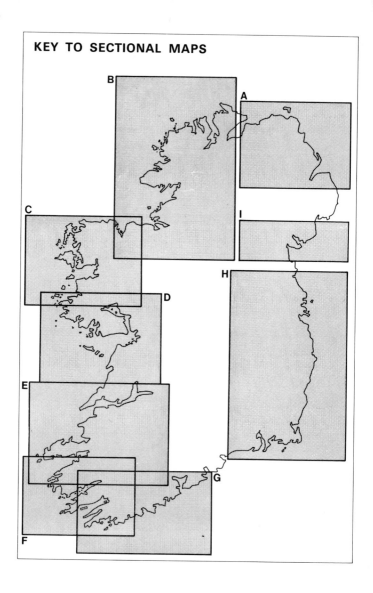

KEY TO SECTIONAL MAPS

B

A

C

I

D

H

E

F

G

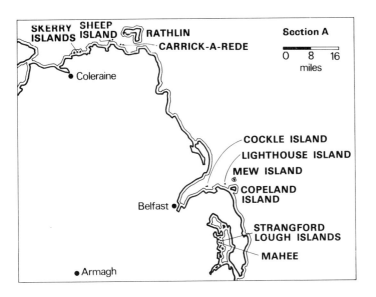

SKERRY
ISLANDS

SHEEP
ISLAND

RATHLIN

CARRICK-A-REDE

Section A

0   8   16
miles

Coleraine

COCKLE ISLAND

LIGHTHOUSE ISLAND

MEW ISLAND

COPELAND
ISLAND

Belfast

STRANGFORD
LOUGH ISLANDS

MAHEE

Armagh

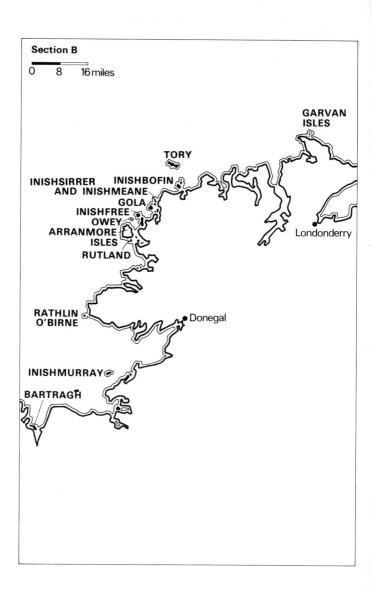

Section B

0   8   16 miles

GARVAN ISLES

TORY

INISHBOFIN

INISHSIRRER
AND INISHMEANE

GOLA

INISHFREE

OWEY

ARRANMORE
ISLES

RUTLAND

Londonderry

RATHLIN
O'BIRNE

Donegal

INISHMURRAY

BARTRAGH

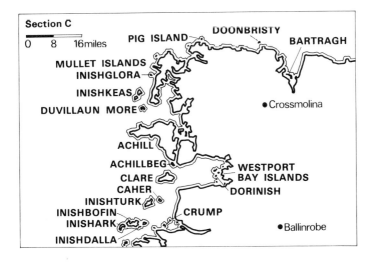

Section C

0 8 16miles

DOONBRISTY

PIG ISLAND

BARTRAGH

MULLET ISLANDS
INISHGLORA

INISHKEAS

DUVILLAUN MORE

● Crossmolina

ACHILL

ACHILLBEG

CLARE

WESTPORT
BAY ISLANDS

CAHER

DORINISH

INISHTURK

INISHBOFIN

CRUMP

INISHARK

INISHDALLA

● Ballinrobe

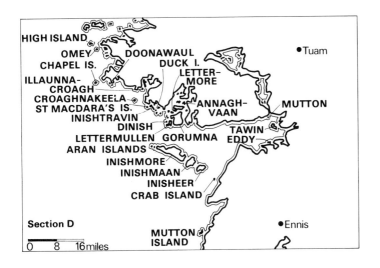

HIGH ISLAND

OMEY

DOONAWAUL

● Tuam

CHAPEL IS.

DUCK I.

ILLAUNNA-
CROAGH

LETTER-
MORE

CROAGHNAKEELA

ANNAGH-
VAAN

MUTTON

ST MACDARA'S IS.

INISHTRAVIN

DINISH

TAWIN

LETTERMULLEN GORUMNA

EDDY

ARAN ISLANDS

INISHMORE

INISHMAAN

INISHEER

CRAB ISLAND

Section D

● Ennis

MUTTON
ISLAND

0 8 16miles

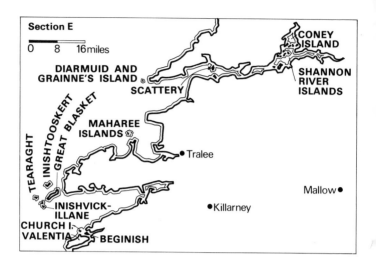

Section E

0   8   16 miles

DIARMUID AND
GRAINNE'S ISLAND
SCATTERY

CONEY
ISLAND
SHANNON
RIVER
ISLANDS

TEARAGHT
INISHTOOSKERT
GREAT BLASKET

MAHAREE
ISLANDS

INISHVICK-
ILLANE
CHURCH I.
VALENTIA
BEGINISH

•Tralee

Mallow•

•Killarney

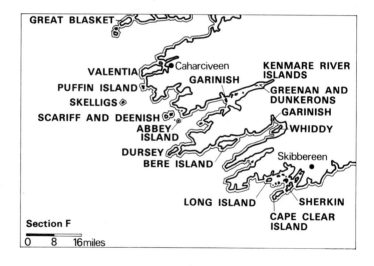

GREAT BLASKET

VALENTIA
PUFFIN ISLAND
SKELLIGS
SCARIFF AND DEENISH
ABBEY
ISLAND
DURSEY
BERE ISLAND

•Caharciveen
GARINISH

KENMARE RIVER
ISLANDS
GREENAN AND
DUNKERONS
GARINISH
WHIDDY

Skibbereen
•

LONG ISLAND
CAPE CLEAR
ISLAND
SHERKIN

Section F

0   8   16 miles

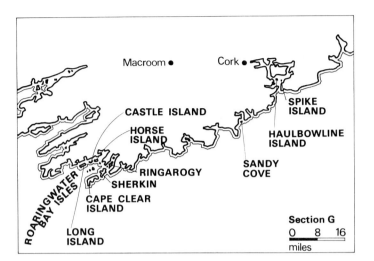

Macroom ●   Cork ●

CASTLE ISLAND   SPIKE
                                 ISLAND

HORSE
ISLAND   HAULBOWLINE
                         ISLAND

RINGAROGY   SANDY
                     COVE
SHERKIN

CAPE CLEAR
ISLAND

LONG   Section G
ISLAND
                     0   8   16

                     miles

ROARINGWATER BAY ISLES

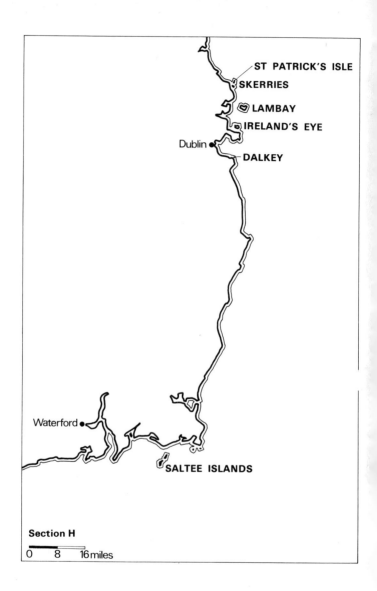

ST PATRICK'S ISLE

SKERRIES

LAMBAY

IRELAND'S EYE

Dublin ●

DALKEY

Waterford ●

SALTEE ISLANDS

Section H

0   8   16 miles

Section I

0   8   16miles

Newry •

BLOCKHOUSE AND
GREEN ISLANDS

B

ABBEY

SITUATION: close inshore, in Derrynane Bay, to Lamb's Head, County Kerry.
AREA: 20 acres.
POPULATION: uninhabited.
ACCESS: at low tide on foot.

Abbey Island is only surrounded by water at high tide. It is low, rocky, and connected to the mainland at low water by a sand-bar. Its chief feature is the ruined Derrynane Abbey, said to have been founded in the 6th century by St Finian. Possibly the original church was built then, but the ruins date back only to the 13th century. Less pleasing are the somewhat vulgarly flamboyant modern gravestones to be found in the vicinity.

See also Kenmare River Islands.

ACHILL

SITUATION: less than $\frac{1}{2}$ mile w. of Achill village on the mainland of County Mayo.
AREA: 57 sq. miles.
POPULATION: 4,500 (1970).
ACCESS: by road bridge across Achill Sound from Achill village.

Since 1888 Achill Island has been linked to the mainland by an iron swivel-bridge, a fact which should strictly rule it out of this book. However, Achill is included because it is the largest island off the Irish coast and it still retains the atmosphere of one.

The whole area is mainly one of bogs and heather, but there is some splendid cliff scenery, and Achill can boast of three mountains, Slievemore (2,204 ft), Croaghaun (2,192 ft) and Minawn (1,530 ft). From each of these peaks excellent views may be obtained, and Croaghaun is particularly impressive in this respect as its sides drop right down to the sea.

One approaches Achill Island from the village of Achill, which in years past was the point from which the ferry trip to the island was made. The road bridge leads across to the village of Achill Sound. Since the erection of the bridge Achill has seen a great increase in the number of visitors, but it is still largely unspoilt and in parts has an air of remoteness, though there are hotels and boarding houses in most parts.

Achill Sound village is where most of the shops are to be found and it is also the place on which the tourist invasion is usually concentrated. Some even come to look at the spot-lit portrait of Brendan Behan which hangs in one of the bars here.

To avoid being immersed in Achill Sound's tourism it is as well to turn off the main road, admiring the masses of rhododendrons along the Sound, and to go s. towards Kildavnet. This is a much more attractive route and takes one past a small, ruined church and an unusual 15th-century tower-house.

At the s. end of the island facing the small island of Achillbeg is a ruined barracks near a ring-fort on the edge of the sea. You can then turn w. along what is known as Atlantic Drive, which is a road running high up above the cliffs. Car bays have been built along here so that one can stop to admire the scenery. At the centre of the island is the village of Keel. This is a favoured resort, with its nine-hole golf course,

2

Achill Island, Keem Bay (Irish Tourist Board)

good bathing, and sands, not to mention the trout-fishing at Lough Keel, a short distance inland. Keel Strand or beach is 3 miles long with firm sands, a shallow sea and a wide bay.

There is much to see in this district of Achill. Nearby are the Minawn cliffs which rise 800 ft sheer from the sea, and at the E. end of the Strand are the Cathedral Rocks, a curious quartzite formation. It is said that in Achill, if you take sufficient pains, you can always bring back with you a chunk of amethyst. Certainly streaks of amethyst have been found in rocks on the island, and there is also an Amethyst Hotel.

Another village not far from Keel is Dooagh, which also has a fine bathing beach. This is a centre for the shark-fishing which has been started up in Achill in recent years. You will see the currachs used for this lying along the shore, with the sharking nets stowed aboard. Shark-fishing is not merely a sport in these parts, but an industry, and the liver is cut from the sharks and the oil extracted.

Ashleam ('The Mountain of the Leap') is worth a visit. It is a village of straggling white cottages with thatched roofs and the pungent smoke of turf fires curling out of chimneys. Then there is St Colman's Knitting Industry where girls are employed making scarves, socks, ties, and other knitted garments.

Achill Head, at the w. extremity of the island, is an incredible blade-sharp double range of cliffs, set back to back, some 378 ft above the sea. It presents a challenging, and dangerous climb for the enthusiast, but the view from the knife-edge parapet along the cliff-tops is magnificent. In many respects it compares with Croaghaun itself, even though the cliffs of the latter form a precipice of 2,000 ft.

Inland from here is some splendid walking country across springy heather-covered upland down to the unexpected little lake of Bunnafreeva, which so impressed the traveller Edward Newman when he visited it in 1838 that he wrote: 'Near the margin of the cliff is a beautiful little fresh water lake, surrounded by an amphitheatre of hills . . . its singularly round form, the depth of the basin in which it reposes, the precipitous sides of that basin, its height above the sea – all these are characters of no ordinary interest.'

The inhabitants of Achill seem to have been apathetic to the monuments of the past, of which there are few, and these in a neglected state and in many instances destroyed by people who have used ancient ruins for building materials. A sandhill settlement and some kitchen middens survive at Trawmore, but these are not remarkable. Even the old church dedicated to St Colman on the road from Keel to Dugort is little more than a pile of stones with a few primitive crosses.

At Dugort on the E. side of Slievemore is the site of the former missionary settlement of Edward Nangle, a bigoted Protestant who in 1832 set up the mission to convert Roman Catholics. The Revd E. Nangle belonged to the Church Missionary Society and the colony he founded totalled about 360 who had been given the stark alternatives of 'bed and board as Protestants, or poverty and starvation as Catholics'. It would seem that he did good work for those he persuaded to give up their religion, but mercilessly pilloried and attacked those who declined to be wooed by his promises. He launched the *Achill Herald* as a vehicle for his propaganda, a violently aggressive news-sheet which stirred up sectarian bitterness. His funds certainly sustained the newspaper and acquired much land in the island, but ultimately his attempt to win converts was a failure. The mission is now a holiday centre.

It was John Porter, of Belleisle, County Fermanagh, who fought for the building of a bridge between Achill and the mainland and eventually, by putting up some of the money himself, saw his dream realised. He was far-sighted enough to see that the island would not survive as an economic entity unless a bridge was built. Today's population figures are proof of his accurate judgement, for while most of Ireland's islands have seen their populations decline over the past hundred years, Achill's is almost the same today as it was in 1891, despite the steady drain of young people from the island to the mainland and England.

The other vital factors in maintaining some kind of prosperity for Achill were the development of its road system in the early 20th century and the establishment of tourism.

Perhaps the prime tourist attraction is that owing to its NW. situation the island has the longest evening daylight in Europe, which encourages people to come here even in spring and autumn.

A number of authors have been attracted to Achill and have used it as a setting for novels – notably Miriam Alexander in *The Ripple*, which has some vivid descriptions of Achill scenery, and Michael Ireland, whose *Children of the Earth* contains an earthy and passionate account of life on the island.

Accommodation: there are hotels at Achill Sound (2), Dugort (2), Keel (3), and Dooagh (2), various boarding houses, and some cottages to let furnished. Camping and caravan sites are available.

Post Offices and banks at Achill Sound, Curraun, Newport, Westport, and some other centres.

Churches: Roman Catholic at Achill Sound, Curraun, Kildownet, Bunnacurry, and Keel; and Church of Ireland at Achill Sound and Dugort.

Books: *This is Ireland* series, by Richard Hayward, Arthur Barker, 1955; *County Guides to Galway, Mayo, Connemara*, Irish Overseas Publishing Co., Tralee; *Children of the Earth*, by Michael Ireland (Darrell Figgis), Mansel & Co., Dublin, 1918.

ACHILLBEG

SITUATION: 250 yds S. of Achill Island, and ½ mile from the mainland of County Mayo.

AREA: 45 acres.
POPULATION: uninhabited.
ACCESS: by boat from Curraun.

A favourite excursion venue for those staying at the Youth Hostel at Carraun, which faces Achillbeg across the water. There is good bathing and in spring and early summer the island is filled with the colourful Mediterranean Heath (*erica*).

ANNAGHVAAN

SITUATION: close inshore to Bealadangan, County Galway, and $\frac{1}{2}$ mile N. of the island of Lettermore.
AREA: 311 acres.
POPULATION: 109.
ACCESS: linked by road bridge to Bealadangan and by bridge and causeway to Lettermore.

Annaghvaan is the first of a series of islands linked together by bridges and causeways off this part of the Galway coast. A road crosses the SE. extremity of Annaghvaan. There is little to see and the terrain is wild and somewhat bleak.

ARAN

SITUATION: 2 miles W. of Burtonport, County Donegal.
AREA: 7 sq. miles.
POPULATION: 869 (1970).

ACCESS: by boat daily except Sundays from Burtonport (in July and August every ½ hr) at 10.00 a.m. and 2.00 p.m. Return fare 20p. Cost of transporting a car is 150p.

The largest of the Aranmore Isles (q.v.), Aran is often called Aranmore to avoid confusing it with the Aran Isles off Galway. Possibly because of its exposed position, Aran has attracted less interest than almost any other island of its size off the Irish coast. Yet Peadar O'Donnell wrote of it: 'Beloved Aranmore, where they are quick to admire your gifts, but where they love you for your faults.'

It is best known for the Aranmore light which stands at an elevation of 233 ft on Rinrawros Point, the NW. extremity of the island. This is the most powerful lighthouse on the Irish coasts. The Aranmore lifeboat rides at anchor off the minute Calf Island and is responsible for rescue work over 200 miles of coast from Malin Head to Eagle Island, off NW. Mayo.

The island itself rises to a height of 734 ft at Cliudamiller in the interior. The W., NE., and part of the S. sides are edged with vertical cliffs, intersected by deep fissures and caves and indented by several small bays. The caves are specially interesting, though some of them are hazardous to explore.

Aran has a varied landscape with rocky headlands, gently sloping valleys, and seven mountain lakes, one at least of which (Lough Shire) contains rainbow trout. The whole area is a centre of the herring fishing which provides employment for many. Cod, tope, dogfish, gurnard, and mackerel can be caught in the sea.

There are no police (guards, as they call them here) on this island with a population of 869, which rises to 2,000 in summer. The fishing fleet comprises thirty half-deckers with four-man crews, and in summer makes Aran seem a far busier place than it really is. To cater for the fishermen and the visitors there are seven pubs on the island, and many modern houses have been built here under the Gaeltacht Housing Scheme. The two schools, at one of which Peadar O'Donnell was headmaster, both have stretches of beach for their playgrounds.

A good deal of Aran is fertile land. It used to be said that every cottage kept a cow, but much of the milk today comes from the mainland, though the islanders graze sheep and cut turf on the hills. Some 200 sheep are lost over the cliffs each year.

The unique pearls known as the 'Four O'Donnell Pearls' are believed to have been hidden on Aran after the departure from Ireland in 1607 of 'Red' Hugh O'Donnell, their original owner. They are now in the possession of Mr Ernest Chapman, of London.

Accommodation: there is an Irish Tourist Board registered hotel on the island and full board can be had in some of the houses. A number of houses are for letting. Youth Hostel.

Post Office.

Churches: Roman Catholic.

Entertainments: 'singing pubs' and dance hall.

Books: *Donegal Annual, No. 5* (1962) contains an article by Mr C. Hargraves on 'Economic and Social Conditions on Aranmore in the 19th & 20th Centuries'; *Aranmore : the Human Touch*, by Eugene Derwent, 1967, available from the Secretary, Aranmore Development Association.

ARAN ISLANDS

SITUATION: 30 miles SW. from Galway, at the entrance
to Galway Bay.
TOTAL AREA: 18 sq. miles.
POPULATION: 1,850 (1970).
ACCESS: by air daily from Galway to Inishmore, or by
boat from Galway to Inishmore, normally 3 times a
week, but more frequently in summer. Inter-island
trips by currach can be arranged from Inishmore.

The Aran Islands, or *Oilean Arann*, meaning the
'Islands of Aran', are steeped in ancient pagan and
Christian history. There are three islands – Inishmore
(q.v.), Inishmaan (q.v.), and Inisheer (q.v.), the
names meaning the Great Island, the Middle Island,
and the South-East Island respectively. They lie in
a straight line from NW. to SE. and form a natural
breakwater for Galway Bay, Inisheer being the closest
to the mainland at a distance of seven miles.

All the islands are composed of a limestone *karst* –
bare platforms of grey rock and green fields surrounded by high stone walls, and interspersed with
the gaily-coloured plants native to limestone. Aran
flowers are one of the best features of the islands,
ranging from mid-winter primroses to cowslips,
gentians, purple cranesbill, white roses, honeysuckle,
wild orchids, harebells, wild thyme, and yellow
centuary, while in the many neat gardens of the
cottagers you will find roses, hollyhocks, gladioli,
and carnations.

The islands were inhabited at a very early date
(*circa* 700–200 BC) by a tribe known as the Fir Bolg,

Inisheer, Aran Islands (Irish Tourist Board)

who fled from the mainland after being defeated at the Battle of Moytura, fought out on the plains of what is today County Sligo. This tribe fortified the islands, and the remains of some of these fortresses can still be seen.

Christianity was brought to the Aran Isles in the 5th century by St Enda, who was originally a chief of the Oriels, but was converted to Christianity. He was given possession of the Aran Islands by his brother-in-law, Aengus, King of Munster, and established a monastic school there. Enda made the Arans famous as a seat of learning so that they were referred to as 'the islands of the Saints'. The school Enda set up became renowned throughout Europe and at one time 3,000 students were in residence.

About the year 1120 a branch of O'Briens, Kings of Munster, became overlords of the islands, but in 1587 Queen Elizabeth put an end to their independence, granting them to John Rawson of Athlone on condition that he maintained twenty soldiers there. Enda's school and the church he built remained until the time of Cromwell, during which the islands became a refuge of Catholic clergy.

The Arans provide a wealth of antiquarian remains both of the prehistoric and early Christian periods – so much so that complete details of them would fill a considerable-sized book. The early forts are of special interest, but there are several examples of early Christian churches, as well as cromlechs, stone crosses, and inscribed murals. Unfortunately Cromwell put a garrison on Inishmore and destroyed a great deal, using stones from the churches to build a castle.

Most of the people are Gaelic-speaking and are engaged in agriculture and fishing. For the latter they use the famous Aran currach, a coracle made of wood slats and tarred canvas. The currach is still built on the island and is an adaptation of the traditional currach of antiquity, when animal hides were stretched across a light wooden frame. The craft has stood the test of time well and, apart from fishing, is used as the chief means of inter-island transport. Normally there are three rowers, but for long trips an outboard motor is operated.

The dress of the inhabitants is quite distinctive – a white homespun waistcoat called a *bainin*, blue-grey tweed trousers, knitted cap, a woven woollen belt called a *crios*, and raw-hide shoes. They are a gay people, and one of the attractions for visitors is the ballad-singing sessions which are held nightly in summer in the island's inns. Irish dances are also held twice weekly in Kilronan. Cliff-climbing, sea-angling (for cod, mackerel, and pollock), and botanical excursions in search of unusual plants are other activities available on the islands.

The film *Man of Aran* was made in the islands by Robert Flaherty, with Barbara Mullen and Maggie Dirane in the leading roles, the picture being based on Liam O'Flaherty's sketches and stories of island life. The Aran Islands have attracted many writers, the most famous being J. M. Synge, who stayed on Inishmaan and wrote his play *Riders to the Sea* about the people of the island. He also found much other material in the Arans for his other works, notably *The Playboy of the Western World* and *The Shadow of the Glen*.

Accommodation: mainly on Inishmore, but there are boarding houses on Inisheer and Inishmaan.

Post Offices and banks: there is a sub-office of the Bank of Ireland in Kilronan (Inishmore), and Post Offices on all three islands.

Books: *The Aran Islands*, by J. M. Synge, Mansel, Dublin and London, 1907, and Oxford University Press, 1962; *Man of Aran*, by Pat Mullen, Faber & Faber, 1934; *Some Irish Yesterdays*, by Somerville (Edith Oenone) and Ross (Violet Martin), Longmans, 1906; *Short Stories and Sketches of Island Life*, by Liam O'Flaherty, Jonathan Cape, 1937; *Connacht : The Counties Galway, Mayo, Sligo, Leitrim and Rosscommon*, by Sean Jennett, Faber & Faber, 1970; *The Aran Isles*, by Daphne Pochin Mould, David & Charles, 1972.

Recording: 'Songs of Aran', recorded by Sidney Robertson Cowell, Ethnic Folkways Library, Album No. FE 4002.

Typical hookers (small fishing craft) seen off the Islands (Irish Tourist Board)

ARANMORE: *see* Aran.

ARANMORE ISLES

SITUATION: $2\frac{1}{2}$–3 miles off the coast of Donegal, about the same distance from Burtonport, and $2\frac{1}{2}$–5 miles from Dungloe.

TOTAL AREA: about 9 sq. miles.

POPULATION: 1,000.

ACCESS: by boat from Burtonport.

14

This is a cluster of islands lying between Crohy Head and Bun Beg, the largest of which is Aran (q.v.), or Aranmore. The islands are known as the Aranmore Isles to distinguish them from the Aran Islands off Galway.

Most of the population is concentrated on Aran, and the principal occupation is fishing, though some farming and grazing is done on a relatively small scale. Gaelic is widely spoken, and a feature of the islands is that almost everyone is called by his Christian name and it is often hard to discover surnames. In July and August the islands become the headquarters of the Irish College, and some 200 Gaelic scholars assemble there for studies and indulge in organised games and *ceilidhs* (song and dance festivals).

The other principal islands in the group are Cruit (which is now linked to the mainland), Rutland (q.v.), Inniscoo, Iochtar, Island Crone, Inishfree (q.v.), and Inniskeragh.

ARDOILEAN: *see* High Island.

AVERY

SITUATION: close to Mason Island, $\frac{1}{4}$ mile to the W. of Mweenish and 2 miles S. of Ard, County Galway.
AREA: 5 acres.
POPULATION: uninhabited.
ACCESS: by boat from Ard.

C

BARTRAGH

SITUATION: in Killala Bay, County Mayo, $\frac{1}{2}$ mile from the mainland.
AREA: 367 acres.
POPULATION: uninhabited.
ACCESS: by boat from Killala.

A long, low-lying, sandbank island, Bartragh shelters Kallala and Moyne Abbey from the wide, outer reaches of Killala Bay. There is some bird life and good bathing; otherwise it is of little interest.

BEAR ISLAND: *see* Bere Island.

BEGINISH

SITUATION: close inshore to Knightstown, Valentia Island, $1\frac{1}{2}$ miles w. of the Iveragh Peninsula, County Kerry.
AREA: 35 acres.
POPULATION: uninhabited.
ACCESS: by ferry boat from Reenard to Knightstown, thence by rowing boat; or by hired boat from Reenard direct.

Close to Valentia Harbour, Beginish is noted for its fine sandy beach and its basaltic rock formation, being one of the few places in sw. Ireland where this is to be found. There are traces of ancient field systems, and many caves in the rocks are worth exploring. A small circular stone house has been excavated here.

BERE ISLAND

SITUATION: in Bantry Bay, County Cork, 1 mile from Castletown, Berehaven.
AREA: $6\frac{3}{4}$ sq. miles.
POPULATION: 200 (1970).
ACCESS: by boat from Castletown.

Sometimes called Bear Island, Bere's importance lies mainly in the past, when it was famous as a military and naval base for the British. During World War I the Allied Fleet used the deep anchorage at Bere as a centre for activities in the Atlantic. The lines of battleships and destroyers anchored in the Sound sailed off to fight the Battle of Jutland. Bere Island was one of the Treaty Ports, and after Irish independence a British destroyer and military base were retained here until 1938. The loss of Bere, which would have been invaluable in the war against U-boats (1939–45), was a cause of bitter dissension between the British and Irish governments.

Much of what is to be found here is a reminder of the presence of British forces years ago – gun emplacements, signal posts, and football fields where the soldiers and sailors played. After the British left the island had something of the atmosphere of a ghost town for some years, and little effort was made to adapt to a new form of life. However, in recent years the Bere Peninsula has been opened to tourists and the island is today being developed for deep-sea fishermen and sailing enthusiasts. In 1947 the Glenans Sailing Centre was formed in France by officers of the Resistance Movement to enable youths in the organisation to get to know each other better through a common interest. Today the Glenans Sailing Centre, based on Baltimore, has two bases on Bere Island, catering for boys below the age of eighteen and girls under nineteen.

The island is also of interest to botanists. On its E. end a wedge-shaped galley grave can be seen.

BININY: *see under* Roaringwater Bay Isles.

BIRD ISLAND (Down): *see* Mahee.

BIRDS' ISLAND (Cork): *see under* Roaring-water Bay Isles.

THE BLASKETS

SITUATION: a group of islands lying from 3 to 6 miles SW. of Slea Head, off the Peninsula of Corcaguiney, County Kerry.
TOTAL AREA: $1\frac{1}{4}$ sq. miles.
POPULATION: uninhabited.
ACCESS: by boat from Dunquin Pier or Dingle Pier, by arrangement.

The Blaskets, though today inhabited only by sea birds and rabbits, have the reputation of having possessed 'the happiest people in the world', and for many years they have attracted the attention of writers who have been inspired by their charm and legends.

Remarkably, people do still go back to the Blaskets both from the mainland and as tourists. Their former inhabitants were mainly fishermen and, like most men of the sea, they were great story-tellers. Perhaps the most famous of these was Maurice O'Sullivan, who wrote a book in Gaelic about the islands, which was translated into English as *Twenty Years Agrowing*.

Below: *Blaskets seen from Slea Head (Irish Tourist Board)*

There are several islands in the Blaskets – some no more than rocks, but others formerly supported inhabitants. The main island is Great Blasket (q.v.), while the other principal islands are Tearaght (q.v.), Inishvickillane (q.v.), Inishtooskert (q.v.), and Yellow. They are really an extension of the mountains of the mainland and some rise in places to 1,000 ft above sea level.

The islands are probably better able to support life than many others off the w. coast of Ireland, and some of them are still used for grazing purposes during the summer season and also for lobster fishing. There is an abundance of peat for fuel.

Communication with the mainland is often difficult as the tiny harbour of Dunquin in County Kerry is exposed to the sw. gales and landing places on the islands are not easily negotiable. This particularly applies to the isles of Inishnabro and Yellow.

The history of the Blaskets is largely lost in legend. There are signs that they were inhabited a thousand years ago, and the remains of a fort suggest the Danes came here. But the islands were little known before 1840, when the Irish from the mainland came here to escape the Great Famine and to take advantage of the fish diet offered them. The area is one of the richest fishing grounds in the whole of Europe. The result of this invasion from the mainland was that the population doubled in the next ten years, and the islands became a sanctuary for Gaelic speakers.

The islands were evacuated in 1953 and the Irish Government re-settled the inhabitants on the mainland. Most of the houses fell into decay, but in recent years a number of these homes (including that of Peig Sayers, another of the island's literary figures) have been restored, thanks to the efforts of Mr Taylor

Collings, an American who is anxious to see the islands developed for tourists.

Books: *Twenty Years Agrowing*, by Maurice O'Sullivan; *The Islandman*, by Tomas O'Crohan; *An Old Woman's Reflections*, by Peig Sayers, all re-published by the Oxford University Press.

BLOCKHOUSE AND GREEN ISLANDS (Down)

SITUATION: in Carlingford Lough, County Down.
AREA: 30 acres.
POPULATION: uninhabited.
ACCESS: by boat from Greenmore to Rostrevor.

Owned by the National Trust and leased to the RSPB, Blockhouse and Green Islands are a nesting site for terns.

BORTREES, The: *see under* Strangford Lough Islands.

CAHER

SITUATION: 5 miles W. of Cross Lough, County Mayo.
AREA: 128 acres.
POPULATION: uninhabited
ACCESS: by boat from Inishturk Island or Cross Lough.

Caher is one of the prettiest and most interesting islands in this region, being easily accessible either from the mainland or from Inishturk (q.v.), 2 miles to the W.

Its true Gaelic name is Illaun-na-Neeve, 'The Island of the Saints', and indeed it appears under this title on the Government Stationery Office Maps published in Dublin. There is a small bay on the E. side of the island which can be used as a landing place in calm weather. Close to the landing place is an early stone cross standing on a hillock, dating from the 7th century when the Irish sculptors first began to carve stone slabs.

An early Celtic monastery on Caher is said to have been founded by St Patrick, but whether or not this is true, it was certainly dedicated to this saint. The two gables of the church are still intact and the side walls are fairly well preserved, and within the church stand six sculptured crosses. Beside the church is a large slab lying on the ground known as St Patrick's Bed, and legend has it that anyone suffering from epilepsy can be cured by spending a night on the slab.

The ruins are situated in a hollow surrounded by grass-covered hillocks, and a wall surrounds the monastic settlement. The island is low-lying on the

E., with a small lake in the interior, but on the w. it rises to a height of 200 ft above sea level, with some spectacular cliffs. Of special interest are the wild geese which inhabit the island.

CALF ISLAND: *see under* Aran.

CAMPLIE, The: *see under* Sheep Island.

CANON ISLAND: *see under* Shannon River Islands.

CAPE CLEAR ISLAND

SITUATION: 2 miles SW. of Sherkin Island and 4 miles sw. of Baltimore, County Cork.
AREA: 3 miles by $1\frac{1}{2}$ miles.
POPULATION: 250.
ACCESS: by ferry from Baltimore from 1 June to 30 September, daily at 2.15 p.m. and 7.00 p.m. from Baltimore, returning from Cape Clear at 3 p.m. and 7.45 p.m.

Lying to the s. of Roaringwater Bay, Cape Clear Island is (apart from Fastnet Rock, 3 miles w.) the most south-westerly land in either the British Isles or Eire. It has a wild and precipitous coast with cliffs that are practically inaccessible at its s. end. The lighthouse on Fastnet can be clearly seen from the island.

There are many early Christian relics on Cape Clear, including an early cross pillar stone, various

Cape Clear Island, South Harbour, County Cork (Irish Tourist Board)

gallauns, and the ruins of an ancient fort. St Ciaran is said to have been born on Cape Clear – certainly he lived here, and probably he was of an era earlier than that of St Patrick. The remains of the old fort bring back memories of the days when the O'Driscolls were rulers of the island: it is called Dun an Oir ('Fort of Gold') and is situated on a rock jutting out from the island. The fort was involved in the rebellion of 1601–2 when the Spaniards under Don Juan del Aquila came to the aid of Irish rebel chieftains, but were defeated in the Battle of Kinsale.

Opposite: *Cape Clear Island: aerial view of the harbour (Daphne Pochin Mould)*

24

Most of the inhabitants are purely Irish-speaking. At one time there were more than 600 of them, but in the 1930s the island's population began to dwindle owing to the decline of the mackerel fisheries. In recent years, however, thanks to tourism, Cape Clear has held its own. There are many attractions for visitors, from bird-watching to fishing, rock-climbing, sailing, and archaeology. As one of West Cork's three Gaeltacht areas the island is visited annually by hundreds of young people who come to learn the Irish language.

A bird-watching station has been established here by Bristol University, and an all-the-year-round watch on migratory birds is now kept.

For many years the inhabitants regarded themselves as 'Capers' and not Irish, insisting on their total independence of the mainland. Indeed not so many years ago they had their own laws and even their own 'king'.

Accommodation: there is limited accommodation on the island, including a Youth Hostel on the South Harbour.

CARNADREELAGH: *see under* Garvan Isles.

CARRICK-A-REDE

SITUATION: close inshore to County Antrim and 5 miles
   sw. of Rathlin Island; nearest town Ballintoy, 2 miles.
AREA: 5 acres.
POPULATION: uninhabited.
ACCESS: by means of the 'swinging bridge', or by hired
   boat from the mainland.

If visiting this part of Northern Ireland, you will
probably be advised to go to Carrick-a-Rede to
enjoy the view. Be warned that, unless you have
strong nerves and a head for heights, your enjoyment
may be impaired if you take the short cut – i.e. by
the frail-looking rope bridge across the 60 ft wide
chasm which separates this island rock from the mainland. The bridge swings perilously as one crosses at a
height of 90 ft above the roaring waves. Bryan Mac-
Mahon in his book *Here's Ireland* says of it, 'if going
out was bad, returning was the refinement of terror.'
   So bear in mind that there is an alternative route
by boat. The views from Carrick-a-Rede are magnificent, the bird life is varied, and the chasm between
island and mainland is an excellent salmon run.

CARRICKBANE: *see under* Garvan Isles.

CARRICKMORE: *see under* Garvan Isles.

CARTHY: *see under* Roaringwater Bay Isles.

CASTLE ISLAND (Antrim): *see under* Skerry
   Islands (Antrim).

CASTLE ISLAND

SITUATION: $\frac{3}{4}$ mile E. of Copper Point in Roaringwater
   Bay, County Cork.
AREA: 120 acres.
POPULATION: 15.
ACCESS: by boat (25 mins) from the Cork mainland.

This privately-owned island has a modern house,
six unconverted cottages, a pier, a sandy beach, and
a good supply of fresh water.
   See also Roaringwater Bay Isles.

CHAPEL ISLAND

SITUATION: 1 mile SW. of the extreme W. tip of Bally-
   conneely Peninsula, County Galway.
AREA: 20 acres.
POPULATION: uninhabited.
ACCESS: by boat from Ballyconneely Bay.

Chapel Island takes its name from the remains of the
tiny Chapel of St Caillin still to be seen here. It also
contains St Caillin's Well.

CHURCH ISLAND (Dublin): *see* St Patrick's
   Isle.

CHURCH ISLAND
(Kerry)

SITUATION: in Valentia Harbour, close to Knightstown, $1\frac{3}{4}$ miles W. of the Iveragh Peninsula, County Kerry.
AREA: 40 acres.
POPULATION: uninhabited.
ACCESS: by ferry boat from Reenard and thence by rowing boat from Knightstown; or by hired boat direct from Reenard.

Situated in the harbour of Valentia Island, Church Island gets its name from the remains of an ancient monastery which existed there. Some beehive cells are to be found, too.

CLARE

SITUATION: $4\frac{1}{2}$ miles NW. of the Coast of County Mayo, at the entrance to Clew Bay, and 17 miles W. of Westport.
AREA: $5\frac{1}{2}$ sq. miles.
POPULATION: 300 (1970).
ACCESS: by boat from Westport Quay or Louisburgh.

Approaching the small harbour on the SE. corner of Clare Island, which is the recognised landing place, the first landmark one sees is the gaunt, square, 16th-century tower known as Grace O'Malley's Castle.

The tower stands on a peninsula overlooking the sheltered bay, and it commemorates the island's folk heroine, Granuaile O'Maile (or O'Malley), chief of the sept of that name in the reign of Elizabeth I. The O'Malley family motto was 'invincible on land and sea', and it was Granuaile's foremost desire to live up to this. She was the sea-queen of the Western Isles; her base was on Clare Island, and she demanded the paying of a toll by all ships, of whatever nationality, which came near Clare.

She was both a queen in her own right and one who, when it suited her, acknowledged Queen Elizabeth. Indeed, so feared and respected was Granuaile that she was received with full honours at the court of the Tudor Queen. Sir Henry Sidney, who met her in 1576 in Galway, stated 'there came to me a most famous feminine sea-captain called Grany Imallye and offered her services to me, whereever I would command her, with 3 galleys and 200 fighting men, either in Ireland or in Scotland. She brought with her her husband, for she was as well by sea as by land more than Mrs Mate with him.'

Grace was married three times. Her first husband was O'Flaherty, Prince of Connemara, whose castle and lands she had to defend for him, so that his home became known as the 'Hen's Castle'. Then she married Sir Richard Burke, bargaining with him beforehand that after a year either party would be free to dissolve the marriage. With cynical resolution Grace speedily infiltrated her retainers and soldiers into her husband's estates and castles on the mainland, and at the end of the year had acquired strong defensive positions there. She then took over his possessions and abruptly dismissed him. About her third husband we know very little.

Unlike many warlike male chieftains of the period, Grace seems to have had the skill to maintain her dominance right up to her death. She was buried in the tiny abbey on Clare, the ruins of which can still be seen. Here, in a recess in the wall, is kept a skull which the islanders claim is that of Grace herself.

Though ruined, the abbey has much of interest preserved in it. There is a stone which bears the O'Maile family motto, an altar tomb, and a plastered ceiling below the chancel roof bearing paintings of various animals, a fascinating example of medieval fresco.

Clare is almost Ireland in miniature – fertile and green, its mood and colours changing with the weather, frequently lit by the most brilliant of rainbows, a mixture of soft, verdant vales, peat bogs, and upland. The highest point on the island is the Knockmore, rising to 1,500 ft, which provides splendid views across the whole area.

The inhabitants are engaged in farming and fishing. The island was bought for £5,000 – a bargain at the price – by the Congested Districts Board and, though it had 587 inhabitants in 1891, has held its own since. Its population figures have never dwindled anything like those of other islands.

There are some superb specimens of alpine plants on the upper slopes of Clare, and various colonies of sea birds. One may also occasionally see the chough, a bird rare in England, with a long red beak and red legs.

St Brigid's Abbey is said to have been founded by the Carmelites in 1224, but this is by no means certain as the original cell in the area was Cistercian.

Clare has a small village in the bay alongside the harbour and this is the main settlement. Crops grown

D

Clare Island, County Mayo (Irish Tourist Board)

on the island include barley and oats and, of course, potatoes, while a large number of sheep can be seen grazing on the hills. Seaweed is the chief manure – it is cut from the rocks at low tide, and then tied and lashed into a flat raft which floats ashore at high tide. The fishing is good, not only in the sea but in the lake and in streams where brown trout abound. Seals frequent the shores at certain periods of the year, and in winter the woodcock is plentiful.

Accommodation: Granuaile Hotel; some cottagers take visitors.
Post Office.
Roman Catholic Church.

Islands in Clew Bay, County Mayo (Irish Tourist Board)

COCKLE ISLAND

SITUATION: close inshore at Groomsport Harbour, County Down.
AREA: 10 acres.
POPULATION: uninhabited.
ACCESS: by special permission.

Cockle Island is a nesting area for terns. It is owned by Mr Gavin Perceval-Maxwell, and managed by the National Trust on an annual agreement.

CONEY (Clare)

SITUATION: in the estuary of the River Fergus, ½ mile offshore from Kiladysert, County Clare.
AREA: 262 acres.
POPULATION: 35.
ACCESS: by boat from mainland.

One of the islands situated in the estuary of the Shannon River (q.v.). In 1966 three families lived on the island.

CONEY (Cork): *see under* Roaringwater Bay Isles.

CONEY (Sligo)

SITUATION: close inshore to Rosses Point, in Sligo Bay.
AREA: 1¼ miles by ½ mile.
POPULATION: 59.
ACCESS: at low tide you may walk or drive across the sand by a posted route; otherwise by boat.

This is a low-lying, flat but verdant isle in a most beautiful setting, with fine views across Sligo Bay and to Knocknarea Mountain, only 1,078 ft high, but in this setting having all the appearance of a majestic peak.

In the narrow channel between Coney Island and Rosses Point is the fixed effigy in metal of a man holding a light which guides ships through at night. The island is a favourite site for picnics and rambling excursions.

COPELAND

SITUATION: 2 miles N. of Donaghadee, County Antrim, and $1\frac{1}{4}$ miles W. of the mainland coast.
AREA: 1 mile long and $\frac{1}{2}$ mile wide.
POPULATION: 25.
ACCESS: by boat from Donaghadee.

Copeland is the largest of the Copeland Islands (q.v.) and the nearest to the mainland. It is a pleasant little island for a day's visit, with a good landing place at an inlet known as Chapel Bay. Close by Chapel Bay is a tiny cemetery containing traces of a chapel which once belonged to the Abbey of Bangor.

The land rises to 88 ft at the NW. end of the island. There is a school, a post office, and a pillar box with the inscription 'ER VII'.

COPELAND ISLANDS

SITUATION: $1\frac{1}{2}-2\frac{1}{2}$ miles N. of County Down, and $2\frac{1}{2}$ miles N. of Donaghadee.
TOTAL AREA: 270 acres.

POPULATION: 25.
ACCESS: by boat from Donaghadee or Groomsport.

A group of three islands which took their name from an English family who settled in Ireland some centuries ago, the Copelands are a favourite area for holiday excursionists from the mainland. The islands are Copeland (q.v.), Lighthouse Island (q.v.), and Mew Island (q.v.).

CRAB ISLAND

SITUATION: 1 mile W. of the village of Fisherstreet, County Clare.
AREA: 3 acres.
POPULATION: uninhabited.
ACCESS: by boat from Fisherstreet.

This isle is mainly rock, and the only interesting fact about it is that about a week before the Irish Rising of 1916, Dowling, the emissary of Sir Roger Casement, who instigated the rising, was landed clandestinely on Crab Island from a German submarine, believing himself to be actually on the mainland. This was the first mishap in a series of catastrophes that led eventually to the arrest of Casement and his subsequent execution by the English.

CROAGHNAKEELA

SITUATION: 3 miles W. of Mace Head, County Galway, and 6 miles SW. of Bertraghboy Bay.
AREA: $\frac{1}{2}$ mile by $\frac{1}{2}$ mile.
POPULATION: uninhabited.
ACCESS: by boat from Ard (4 miles).

This is a hump of an island with a hill 211 ft high in the centre and a well on the S. side. It was formerly inhabited by a few people.

CRUIT ISLAND: *see under* Aranmore Isles *and* Owey.

CRUMP

SITUATION: $\frac{3}{4}$ mile N. of Rinvyle promontory, near Tully Cross, County Galway.
AREA: 30 acres.
POPULATION: uninhabited.
ACCESS: by boat from Rinvyle.

The island contains the remains of an ancient church.

DALKEY

SITUATION: 300 yds off Sorrento Point and 3 miles SE.
of Dun Laoghaire, Dublin Bay.
AREA: 22 acres.
ACCESS: by hired boat from Colliemore Harbour, 20p.

Dalkey is the largest of a group of rocky islets off this part of the coast. It takes its name from the Viking *Dalk eyja* ('Thorn Island') and has the same name in the Irish language, Deilig Inis.

There is a reasonably well-preserved early Celtic chapel on Dalkey, that of St Begnet, the ruins of which are scheduled as a national monument. Its chief features are a massively lintelled doorway, a rock with a ringed cross carved in relief in front of the door, and (a later addition) a bell cote. Nearby is a martello tower, and the men who built this converted the E. end of the chapel into living quarters.

A favourite place for picnic trips for Dublin holiday-makers, Dalkey is inhabited, but often on a part-time basis, so that accurate assessments of the population are difficult. The centuries-old custom of crowning a 'King of Dalkey' is still carried on in carnival spirit with games and other festivities each summer. A local man is elected 'King', he appoints ambassadors to other non-existent realms, and a jolly day out is had by all.

Post Office.

Books: *Proceedings of the Royal Irish Academy*, vol. 24 (1902–4), page 195.

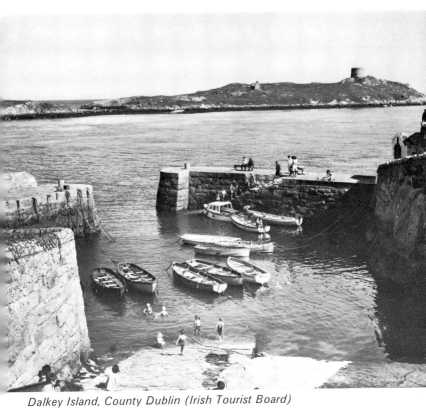

Dalkey Island, County Dublin (Irish Tourist Board)

DEENISH: *see* Scariff and Deenish.

DEER: *see under* Shannon River Islands.

DEILIG INIS: *see* Dalkey.

DIARMUID AND GRÁINNE'S ISLAND

SITUATION: $\frac{1}{4}$ mile off Loop Head, County Clare.
AREA: 3 acres.
POPULATION: uninhabited.
ACCESS: by boat from Loop Head.

A miniature rocky island at the end of the Loop Peninsula, the interest of which lies mainly in its name. Diarmuid and Gráinne are legendary Irish figures, said to have been sun-god and sun-goddess, who fell in love with one another; there are in various parts of Ireland their 'bed', 'grave', and 'cave'.

However, with that delightful inconsequentiality typical of so many Irish names and legends, this particular island has nothing whatsoever to do with this pair. The story linked with it is that of a warrior named Cuchulainn, who was chased by a witch named Mal who had become enamoured of him. He fled from her across the length and breadth of Ireland until he came to Loop Head. Then he hoped to escape from her by jumping across the water to the island. Mal followed him and Cuchulainn immediately jumped back to the mainland. Mal tried to go back after him, but fell into the sea and was drowned. Her body was washed up in what is now called Mal Bay, which is how Milltown Malbay got its name.

DINISH (Galway)

SITUATION: most northerly of the group of 10 islets surrounding Lettermullen Island, 2 miles s. of Ardmore Point, County Galway.
AREA: $\frac{1}{2}$ mile by $\frac{1}{4}$ mile.
POPULATION: uninhabited.
ACCESS: by boat from Lettermullen.

DINISH ISLAND (Kerry): *see under* Kenmare River Islands.

DOG ISLAND: *see under* Lettermullen.

DOONAWAUL

SITUATION: close inshore off the w. extremity of Ballyconneely Peninsula, County Galway.
AREA: 3 acres.
POPULATION: uninhabited.
ACCESS: by boat from Ballyconneely Bay.

The island contains some interesting *clochans* (stone structures).

DOONBRISTY

SITUATION: lying close inshore off the tip of Down-
patrick Head, County Mayo.
AREA: 7 acres.
POPULATION: uninhabited.
ACCESS: by boat from Bunatrahir Bay.

More a rock than an islet, Doonbristy has been
detached from Downpatrick Head's sandstone cliffs
by the action of the sea over the centuries. It is a
curious pear-shaped island, interesting for the remains of a fort perched precariously at its summit,
from which it takes its name. The remains are
almost inaccessible except by helicopter.

DORINISH

SITUATION: 6 miles off Westport, County Mayo.
AREA: 25 acres.
POPULATION: 25.
ACCESS: by rowing boat or motor dinghy from Westport.

A normally uninhabited island which has recently
become the preserve of that phenomenon of modern
life – a commune. When the tide is out its acreage is
seemingly quite large, but at high tide it is well
below 20 acres. From a distance, as you row out to
it from Westport, the curling smoke from open-air
fires and the tents perched on the side of a rock

lend Dorinish a romantic atmosphere. The inhabitants, or commune, call themselves the 'Tribe of the Sun', and for initiative, courage, and determination in selecting a remote and relatively unproductive island as their home they must be praised.

In 1969 the island was purchased and given to the Diggers' Action Group by the pop musician, John Lennon. Shortly after this some thirty people landed there to set up a commune. They have survived for more than two years, but are faced with the problem of wells running dry. Careful cultivation has enabled them to grow vegetables as well as to breed chickens. There is, however, good fishing from the island, providing the inhabitants with oysters, scallops, winkles, and conger eels.

See also Westport Bay Islands.

DUCK ISLAND

SITUATION: 1 mile S. of Mweenish Island off the coast of Galway.
AREA: 20 acres.
POPULATION: uninhabited.
ACCESS: by boat from Mweenish Island.

DUFF ISLAND: *see under* Roaringwater Bay Isles.

DUNKERRONS, The: *see* Greenan and the Dunkerrons.

DUNSEY ROCK: *see under* Strangford Lough
Islands.

DURSEY

SITUATION: close inshore to Crow Head, Bere Peninsula,
County Cork.
AREA: 4 miles by $1-\frac{1}{2}$ mile.
POPULATION: 566.
ACCESS: the island is now linked to the mainland by
cable car.

It is surprising to find a somewhat desolate and
exposed island like Dursey connected by a cable car
to the mainland, but this move, made in 1970, has
opened it up to tourists. It also has two landing places
for those approaching the island by boat, the chief
of these being the harbour at Ballynacallagh on the
NE. side.

There are three tiny villages where the mode of
life is quite unchanged by the coming of tourists.
Farming and fishing are the principal occupations.

Dursey is a rounded hump of land, part of which
contains arable terrain. A trip to Tellickafine on the
far western end of Dursey should not be missed.
The road here passes over the top of Faill a Chiabhine
and provides on a clear day one of the finest views of
this part of Ireland.

There are the remains of two early churches and
an O'Sullivan castle which was destroyed by the
English in 1602. The notable Irish scholar, Don

Dursey Island, County Kerry (Barnaby's Picture Library)

Philip O'Sullivan Bere, who wrote *Ireland Under Elizabeth* (in Latin, Lisbon, 1621), was born here in 1590.

Accommodation: a limited amount is available, as some cotttagers take in visitors.

DUVGLAS: *see under* Garvan Isles.

DUVILLAUN MORE

SITUATION: 3 miles WSW. of Mullet Peninsula, County
   Mayo.
AREA: 1 mile by $\frac{1}{2}$ mile.
POPULATION: uninhabited.
ACCESS: by boat from Fallmore.

This island was inhabited up to the late 1920s,
fishing being the people's main occupation.

Duvillaun More means 'The Black Island'. Its
most interesting landmark is the Crucifixion Slab,
the earliest and one of the most impressive of its
kind, dating probably from the 7th century. There are
also the ruins of an early monastery with a stone
oratory and beehive cells.

EAGLE ISLAND

SITUATION: 3 miles SW. of Erris Head, County Mayo.
AREA: 20 acres.
POPULATION: 3.
ACCESS: by boat from Termoncarragh (4 miles).

This small island reaches a height of 150 ft above sea
level, which makes it an admirable site for the light-

Opposite: *Eagle Island, County Mayo, which receives some
of the roughest seas off the Irish coast: note the breakwater
wall around the lighthouse (Daphne Pochin Mould)*

house, whose group-occulting light is visible for 20 miles. It is well worth a visit, though no longer a sure place to see the eagles which formerly inhabited it.

Eagle Island also provides a radio beacon for aircraft.

EAST CALF: *see under* Roaringwater Bay Isles.

EAST DUNKERRON: *see under* Greenan and the Dunkerrons.

EDDY

SITUATION: $4\frac{1}{2}$ miles S. of the entrance to Galway Harbour, County Galway, and 2 miles W. of the mainland.
AREA: 90 acres.
POPULATION: uninhabited.
ACCESS: by boat from the mainland.

A long, low-lying island, never reaching more than 21 ft in height above sea level, and considerably reduced in size at high water. At low tide sand shoals extend it to very close to the coast.

FIR LANDS: *see under* Garinish (Cork).

48

FURNACE

SITUATION: 1 mile W. of Gorumna Island and 3 miles
    S. of Ardmore Point, County Galway.
AREA: 1 mile by $\frac{1}{2}$ mile.
POPULATION: uninhabited.
ACCESS: by boat from Lettermullen.

The largest of the ten islets which surround Lettermullen Island (q.v.).

GABBOT: *see under* Strangford Lough Islands.

GARINISH (Cork)

SITUATION: 1 mile from the mainland in an inlet of
    Glengarriff Bay, in the innermost section of Bantry Bay,
    County Cork.
AREA: 37 acres.
POPULATION: 5.
ACCESS: by boat from Glengarriff.

Sometimes spelt Garnish, Garinish is also known as
Illnaculin ('Island of the Hollies'). It is one of the
most beautiful small islands off the Irish coast, thanks
to the love and imagination invested in it by the
creator of a wonderful garden here, which transforms
Garinish into a floral paradise with Grecian temples,
miniature Japanese trees, lily ponds, rock gardens,
and shrubberies.

Around Garinish are four rocky islets known as Fir Lands. It is sheltered from the N. and W. by the Caha Mountains and in consequence has a mild climate. 'Such things only happen in fairy tales,' wrote H. V. Morton of Garinish.

Here, facing the Atlantic Ocean, marooned in the wildest and most primitive portion of Southern Ireland, is a perfect Italian garden with pergolas, rock gardens, a marble pond full of gold fish, Roman statues on marble pedestals, sombre cone-shaped cypress trees and every conceivable flower and flowering shrub. It might have been blown over from the hills around Florence on the wings of some magic gale.

Yet in 1796, when the Irish Nationalist leader Wolfe Tone sailed into Bantry Bay with 15,000 troops, and arms which he had persuaded the French Government to send to help Ireland free herself from English rule, Garinish was only a rock, barren except for some gorse and heather. It was deserted except when people came from the mainland to cut turf for fuel.

Storms scattered the fleet which Tone had hoped would rescue Ireland from English bondage, but this incident may have prompted the English to build a martello tower on the island in 1800. The tower is still intact, but the fort, which was built at the same time, has fallen into ruins and has been partly demolished.

For some years into the 19th century Garinish remained a military fortress garrisoned by British troops. In 1910, after it had lain derelict for years, the island was acquired by Annan Bryce, brother of Viscount Bryce and for many years a British MP for a Scottish constituency. He bought it because his wife had fallen in love with it, and together they set about making their 'dream garden'. Earth to cover the bare sandstone rocks had to be brought over from the mainland, and Mr Bryce commissioned an eminent landscape gardener and architect, Mr Harold Peto, of Somerset, to plan his Italian gardens. For more than three years a hundred men worked on the gardens, the Casita, and the Temple. War interrupted the work, and the mansion which was to have been built was never even started.

Annan Bryce died in 1924, but his widow lived on in a cottage on the island with her son, and continued to develop and plant the gardens. Mrs Bryce died in 1939 and her son, Mr Rowland l'Estrange Bryce, inherited the property. By this time the planting of shelter trees had begun to serve its purpose, and it was at last possible to plant many of the rare and interesting trees, shrubs, and flowers – especially magnolias, camellias, and rhododendrons – which now abound there.

Mr Bryce junior continued to adorn the island with exotic plants collected from all over the world, including Japan, China, Central and South America, Australia, New Zealand, South Africa, and the Mediterranean. Because of its sheltered position and the influence of the Gulf Stream, winters on the island are exceptionally mild, though rainfall is high.

Mr Rowland Bryce died in 1953 and bequeathed Garinish to the nation. Today it is administered by the Commissioners of Public Works, and during the summer thousands of people come from Glengarriff to see the gardens.

It was on Garinish that George Bernard Shaw wrote *Saint Joan*.

Italian Garden in Garinish, County Cork (Irish Tourist Board)

Accommodation: none. The island is open to visitors from 10.00 a.m. to 5.30 p.m. on weekdays and from 1.00 p.m. to 5.30 p.m. on Sundays. Landing fee: $12\frac{1}{2}$p for adults and 5p for children.

Books: *In Search of Ireland*, by H. V. Morton, Methuen, 1930.

GARINISH (Kerry)

SITUATION: close inshore to Parknasilla, County Kerry.
AREA: 60 acres.
POPULATION: 3.
ACCESS: by boat from Parknasilla.

Not to be confused with the more celebrated Garinish off County Cork. Nevertheless it, like the other Garinish, is noted for its gardens. It is beautifully wooded and privately owned. Palm trees flourish here in the mild climate and the warmth of the Gulf Stream. Gar Inis means 'the near island', which explains why so many islets around the Irish coast, many of them too tiny to be detailed, have this name.

See also Kenmare River Islands.

GARNISH: *see* Garinish (Cork).

GARRILAUNS, The: *see under* Roaringwater Bay Isles.

GARVAN ISLES

SITUATION: $1\frac{1}{2}$ miles NNE. of Minad Point and $2\frac{1}{2}$ miles E. of Malin Head, County Donegal, the most northerly point of Ireland.
TOTAL AREA: 60 acres.
POPULATION: uninhabited.
ACCESS: by boat from Malin Head.

The Garvan Isles are comprised of several tiny islets and rocks ranging from 40 to 65 ft high, interspersed with numerous sunken rocks and shoals, making an approach to them hazardous. The northernmost island is White Island (40 ft); others are Green Island (65 ft) on the s. end of the group, Middle Island, close to Green on its N. side, Duvglas, Scarony, Carrickbane, Carrickmore, and Carnadreelagh. There are a number of lesser shoals and rocks, but those mentioned are the only ones with any surface area worth mentioning at high tide. Some of the islands are occasionally used for sheep grazing in summer.

GOAT ISLAND: *see under* Roaringwater Bay Isles.

GOLA

SITUATION: $2\frac{1}{2}$ miles NW. of Bunbeg, County Donegal.
AREA: 500 acres.
POPULATION: 10.
ACCESS: by boat from Inishfree Bay.

Gola's population has been declining for several years, though not as fast as those of some of the remoter islands of Ireland. Indeed, over the past 200 years it has seen periods of rise and of fall – rising from 70 in 1841 to 200 in 1930, quite against the national trend, but then declining again in the late 1930s.

Gola lies in Gweedore Bay, and is in many parts a

mass of rugged grey Rosses granite, particularly at Mweelmurrinagh and Mweelmore, at 200 ft the island's highest points. There are pockets of peat deposit in the rock hollows at the N. end and in the E., but these have been extensively cut for fuel. Thus the farming resources of the island are extremely limited, and have in the past been used mainly for grazing cattle. The principal occupation of the Golans was fishing. Kelp was also collected there.

Gola has a heavy rainfall and a long, wet stormy winter, but it is still visited by many in summer, and tributes are then paid to its rugged beauty. It has a pier at Teanmullane on the E. coast and an attractive bay sheltered by Mweelmurrinagh and Mweelmore on the W. The main settlement was on the E. side.

There is a post office on the island, and the few remaining houses are in its vicinity, not far from the stone pier. But there is neither shop, pub, nor church on the island. Gola is almost unique for its size in never having had a church, the inhabitants always having gone to worship on the mainland when the weather permitted, which in winter it frequently does not.

It is not surprising that many of the islanders have moved to the mainland, though some of them retain homes on Gola for the summer. Thus, although the normal population of the island is ten, in June the number sometimes increases to thirty. It is this seasonal addition to the population which explains the presence of eleven currachs, four longboats, and three salmon boats (1969).

In 1838 Lord George Hill purchased an estate in the area, including Gola, and carried out a whole series of reforms. In 1841 he made this report on the area:

It often happens that a man has 3 dwellings – one in the mountains, another upon the shore and the third upon an island [Gola], he and his family flitting from one to another of these habitations, as the various and peculiar herbiage of each is thought to be beneficial to the cattle, which are supposed, at times, to have a disease requiring a change of pasture. . . . The island of Gola is the largest of the four belonging to Lord G. Hill, having 150 inhabitants on it. Owing to the people's Arab mode of life, not having a fixed residence, no pains are taken to make any one of their habitations at all comfortable.

See also Inishsirrer and Inishmeane.

Books: *Gola : The Life and Last Days of An Island Community*, by F. H. Aalen and H. Brody, Mercier Press, Cork, 1969. (This book was sponsored by Radio Telfis Eireann, which made a film about Gola.)

GOLAM HEAD: *see under* Lettermullen.

GORUMNA

SITUATION: 1 mile W. of the mainland of County Galway at the SW. tip of Galway Bay.

AREA: 16 sq. miles.

POPULATION: 1,540.

ACCESS: by boat from Carraroe Quay or Doleen Harbour, or by road bridge on the roundabout route from Bealadangan on the mainland, and then by a series of bridges and over the small islands of Annaghvaan and Lettermore.

Gorumna Island: the Quay at Maumeen (Irish Tourist Board)

If we were to follow the general rule of this book rigidly and omit every island which is linked by bridge and road to the mainland, several Irish islands of importance and interest would be left out. In this corner of Ireland there are four islands linked together by road and causeway – Gorumna, Annaghvaan (q.v.), Lettermore (q.v.), and Lettermullen (q.v.).

Despite these links, they remain islands in spirit and atmosphere. Gorumna is the largest of them, and in parts is remote and lonely. Gaelic is the language mainly spoken, and the children all speak it among themselves and are taught Gaelic as well as English in the schools. It is also worth noting that the links with the mainland have not brought an influx of tourists to Gorumna: perhaps the landscape is too sombre and dull for them. Certainly it does not compare favourably with the magnificent mountain scenery of nearby Connemara.

The most interesting features of Gorumna are its four lakes: one in the N., Lough Illauntrasna, close to the settlement at Teeranea; two close together in the centre; and one on the W., facing Lettermore Island. There is fishing, and scope for a variety of walks, but otherwise little of note on this large but rather monotonous island. What is of importance, however, for the devotee of islands is that it makes an admirable centre for exploring some twenty or thirty islets – most too small to be recorded here – in the immediate vicinity and especially to the W. of Gorumna.

Accommodation: there is an inn on the E. side of Gorumna, close to the bridge link with the island of Lettermullen.

GREAT BLASKET

SITUATION: the largest of the Blaskets group of islands, $2\frac{1}{2}$ miles from Slea Head, County Kerry.
AREA: 5 miles long by 1 mile wide.
POPULATION: uninhabited.
ACCESS: by boat from Dunquin.

Probably no small island, and certainly no remote island in the world has produced three such eminent writers as Great Blasket has given us in Peig Sayers, Maurice O'Sullivan, and Thomas O'Crohan. All of them wrote in Gaelic, and all were inspired by the lives of the island community from which they came. Fortunately for posterity they have all been translated into English, in which language the vividness of their prose and the power of their idioms and symbolism are well preserved. Their descriptions of the vanished way of life on the now uninhabited Great Blasket have become Irish classics, and they have also inspired the work of such scholars as Robin Flower, of England, Karl Marstrander, of Germany, and Professor von Sydow, of Sweden, all of whom have translated their works.

Great Blasket is an island imbued with an aura of the romance of the past, of an era when it was said that the happiest people in the world lived on the island. It is also rich in archaeological interest, and still attracts many visitors for its natural beauties and splendid beaches.

It is not always easy to reach Great Blasket, and sometimes it is impossible for weeks on end. The landing place is in a narrow creek between rocks which have been linked by a cement wall.

The sea is treacherous around this part of the Irish coast, and the rock on which the *Santa Maria*, one of the Spanish Armada vessels, was sunk can still be seen. It is known by fishermen as 'the auld one', and they used to throw plugs of tobacco to appease it as they sailed past.

As one approaches the landing place the ruined homes of the former inhabitants can be seen. But all is not desolation: there are fields of moss and wild flowers, the White Strand, a glorious stretch of sandy beach, seals basking in the bay, and a feeling, on landing, that one has stepped onto the top of a mountain that has poked its head suddenly above the sea. And some people are still known to spend the summer in the ruined houses and thoroughly to enjoy the experience.

In 1920 there were still about 250 people living on Great Blasket, with 1,000 sheep and thirty cows, but curiously no bull. Apparently the cows were taken to the mainland for mating. There were also some thirty horses. There was a 'King' of Great Blasket in those days, and his name was Patrick Kane. Negley Farson, the author described him as 'a fine king. He has a grand face, broad and big, pale with red freckles and bright blue eyes. . . . He had lived on this tiny island all his life . . . and yet when he laughed, it was the laugh of a man who knew the world.'

Gaelic was always spoken on the island, and for many years students came to stay on Great Blasket to learn the language. The last of the islanders left in 1954. Emigration to America had already caused their numbers to decline, but it was the young, anxious to make their way in the world, who finally decided the issue.

There are indications on the island that people lived there a thousand years ago, but much of the history of the island is lost in legend and the story-telling of the natives who were wont to embellish fact in the most extraordinary manner. But there are the remains of two ancient churches on the island.

Great Blasket rises to a height of 900 ft in Croagh Martin, its chief hill, separated by a valley from another hill almost as high, Slieve Donagh. Slieve Donagh has the remains of a fort on its summit – an unusual construction with two separate enclosures. But there are no adequate records of its history.

60

It is not easy to visualise life as it used to be on the island except from the works of the three writers already mentioned. It was informal, haphazard, and yet gay and uninhibited. Thomas Mason, who visited the island in the 1930s, said that 'on summer evenings the younger boys play football and the older lads and the girls dance to the music of melodeon or fiddle. On wet Sunday evenings they adjourn to Old Peg's House, which is locally called "The Dail" or talking place.'

All burials from the island were made on the mainland, as many as eighteen currachs accompanying the coffin in a funeral procession across the bay. As one of the old islanders, now living in Dunquin, said, 'we were sad together and gay together. We had dancing every night. It was fishing and work all day and happy in the night.'

Perhaps the real epitaph to the folk of Great Blasket is to be found in the Gaelic inscription on O'Crohan's grave in Dunquin: 'The likes of us will never be again.'

See also Blaskets, The.

Books: *The Islandman* by Thomas O'Crohan; *Twenty Years Agrowing*, by Maurice O'Sullivan; *An Old Woman's Reflections*, by Peig Sayers; *The Islands of Ireland*, by Thomas H. Mason, Mercier Press, Cork, rev. edn. 1967; *The Western Island or the Great Blasket*, by Robin Flower, Oxford University Press, 1944.

GREAT SALTEE: *see under* Saltee Islands.

GREENAN AND THE DUNKERRONS

SITUATION: Greenan is close inshore on the N. side of the Kenmare River, $3\frac{1}{2}$ miles W. of Kenmare, County Kerry. The Dunkerrons (East and West) are $\frac{3}{4}$ mile from either shore, 2 miles W. of Kenmare.
AREA: Greenan is 20 acres, the Dunkerrons each $\frac{1}{2}$ mile long and about 200 yds wide.
POPULATION: uninhabited.
ACCESS: by boat from either side the river.

At low water Greenan is linked to the mainland and can be reached on foot. The two Dunkerrons are separated by less than 100 yds of water. There are splendid views from all these islands and fishing in the vicinity is good.

See also Kenmare River Islands.

GREEN ISLAND (Donegal): *see under* Garvan Isles.

GREEN ISLAND (Down): *see* Blockhouse and Green Islands.

GREENS ISLAND (Cork): *see under* Roaringwater Bay Isles.

HARE: *see under* Roaringwater Bay Isles.

HAULBOWLINE ISLAND

SITUATION: in Cork Harbour immediately opposite the beach.
AREA: 50 acres.
POPULATION: 431.
ACCESS: by permission of the Irish Naval Command for the area.

Haulbowline Island is the headquarters of the Irish Naval Service. It has steel mills and a dockyard. On the S. and W. sides of the entrance to the basin are two red fixed lights.

HEN ISLAND: *see under* Strangford Lough Islands.

HIGH ISLAND

SITUATION: 4 miles S. of Inishbofin and 2 miles W. of Cleggan Peninsula, County Galway.
AREA: 50 acres.
POPULATION: uninhabited.
ACCESS: by boat from Inishbofin.

A bleak, rocky island with little to offer, High Island (also known as Ardoilean) is nevertheless traditionally

F

said by local legend to 'protect' anyone who gets marooned there. This legend developed when a woman cutting seaweed from a rock was marooned there many years ago. She not only gave birth to a child but, so the story goes, found food of some kind or another awaiting her each day until she was rescued a week later.

There are the ruins of a church, cells, cross-incised slabs, and an enclosing cashel wall on High Island, which is reputed to have been the site of the 7th-century monastic foundation of St Feichin of Fore. St Gormall, known as the Chief Confessor of Ireland, died and was buried here in 1017.

Books: *Journal of the Royal Society of Antiquaries of Ireland*, vol. 36 (1896).

HORSE ISLAND (Clare): *see under* Shannon River Islands.

HORSE ISLAND (Cork): *see under* Roaring-water Bay Isles.

ILLAUNIMMIL: *see under* Maharee Islands.

ILLAUNNACROAGH

SITUATION: 3 miles WNW. of Mace Head, County Galway.
AREA: 18 acres.
POPULATION: uninhabited.

ACCESS: difficult, except in good weather, from Gorteen Bay, 3 miles to the N.

A rocky, isolated island situated hazardously close to the Sunk Bellows and other dangerous visible and submerged rocks in the area.

ILLAUN-NA-NEEVE: *see* Caher.

ILLAUNTANNIG: *see under* Maharee Islands.

ILLNACULIN: *see* Garinish (Cork).

INISHANIER: *see under* Strangford Lough Islands.

INISHARK

SITUATION: 1 mile W. of Inishbofin and 9 miles W. of Cashleen, County Galway.
AREA: 615 acres.
POPULATION: 40 (1970).
ACCESS: by boat from Inishbofin or from the mainland.

Geologically this island is of interest, consisting of ancient metamorphic rocks, gneiss, and schists. It has some grazing land, but the population depends mainly for its services and supplies on the nearby island of Inishbofin.

Inishark, County Galway (Daphne Pochin Mould)

INISHAROAN: *see under* Strangford Lough Islands.

INISHBEG: *see under* Roaringwater Bay Isles.

INISHBOFIN

SITUATION: 8 miles w. of Cashleen, County Galway.
AREA: $3\frac{3}{4}$ sq. miles.
POPULATION: 691.

ACCESS: by boat from Cleggan Bay. The mail boat goes 4 days a week. Normally there is another boat which sails daily and allows 4 hrs on the island.

There is a long, complicated, typically embellished Irish legend as to how Inishbofin got its name: translated, it means 'The Island of the White Cow'. The story varies according to who happens to be telling it, but briefly it concerns two fishermen lost at sea who landed on Inishbofin and found there an old witch chasing a white cow with a stick. The Royal Society of Antiquaries records in its *Antiquarian Handbook* this statement by the late Mr T. J. Westropp: 'The horrified fishermen, indignant at the presence of the witch, struck her and at once became rocks.'

St Colman is the patron saint of Inishbofin. He was a bishop of the Irish missionary settlement at Lindisfarne in Northumberland who returned to Ireland in the 7th century and founded a monastic settlement here.

Today it is a major centre for lobster fishing. Inishbofin has a mile-long inlet making a splendid natural harbour which in Tudor and Cromwellian times was of some importance. Prior to that it had been a resort of pirates. During the Cromwell era Inishbofin was used for the transportation of priests and monks and its castle was taken by Cromwell, who fortified it considerably. Later it was garrisoned by William III against possible French invasion.

Bosco's Castle stands at the entrance to the harbour. It was probably built about the 15th century and greatly extended and rebuilt in the 16th century. Little is known of Bosco except that he was a Spanish pirate of particularly ruthless chracter. He had a

67

Inishbofin, County Galway (Daphne Pochin Mould)

chain placed across the harbour, and anyone who managed to land without his permission was thrown into the sea.

Little, unfortunately, has been done to preserve Inishbofin's ancient heritage: there are traces of the ruin of a medieval church, with a graveyard that has been totally neglected and is covered with weeds and nettles. The inhabitants call it 'The Monastery'. The modern Roman Catholic church is situated near the harbour, and there is a resident priest on the island who also looks after the nearby island of Inishark (q.v.).

Inishbofin is a fertile island, with a deep deposit of boulder clay. Its cattle are particularly good, and the life of the inhabitants is of a higher standard than on most islands off the w. coast of Ireland. Despite the fact that there are few trees, bird life is varied, partly because the island is dotted with a number of small but attractive lakes. Wheatear, wren, starling, oyster-catcher, lark, stonechat, ringed plover, curlew, common tern, heron, fulmar, cormorant, guillemot, wood pigeon, and raven are all to be found here. Seals are also plentiful.

There are some excellent beaches, and the whole area makes an admirable venue for a quiet holiday.

The name Inishbofin is pronounced as though it had two f's, and it is said that the islanders have an unusual manner of speech which is known locally as 'Bofin Irish'.

Accommodation: there is one hotel on the island, and some cottagers take in visitors.

Post Office.

Books: *The Islands of Ireland*, by Thomas H. Mason, Mercier Press, Cork, rev. edn. 1967; *This is Ireland* series, by Richard Hayward, Arthur Barker, 1955.

INISHDALLA

SITUATION: close inshore to Inishbofin and Inishark Islands, off the coast of Galway.

AREA: 50 acres.

POPULATION: uninhabited.

ACCESS: from Inishark or Inishbofin.

Inishdalla means 'The Island of Cattle', and the island is used for grazing by the inhabitants of Inishark (q.v.).

INISHEER

SITUATION: one of the Aran Islands, 6 miles NW. of Fisherstreet in County Clare.
AREA: $2\frac{1}{4}$ sq. miles.
POPULATION: 350 (1970).
ACCESS: by boat from Fisherstreet, or by the 'Islander' plane to Inishmore, the main island of the group, and thence by boat.

Inisheer, one of the Aran Islands (q.v.), deserves more attention from archaeologists than it has so far received, for it possesses two small tumuli, several early churches with graveyards and inscribed stones, a holy well, the remains of a fort, a medieval castle, a stone cairn, and a large kitchen midden. Nevertheless it is only fair to mention the fact that so far archaeologists have not exactly been encouraged to carry out excavations. Local superstition about tampering with relics of the past is strong, and stories are told of dire ailments and even death which have visited those who have dug on the island.

But these remains are well worth exploring. What the locals call the 'kitchen midden' is the dumping ground used by the early coast-dwellers, who mainly ate shell-fish, and dumped the shells with bones and other refuse in a walled area about 100 yds long and 50 yds wide. High up on the island is the remaining structure of the Church of St Keevan, almost covered in sand. On 14 June each year the islanders clear the sand from the interior of the building, place lighted candles there, and pray during the night.

This is a limestone island, with bare platforms of

grey rock interspersed with green fields protected by high stone walls. Flowers flourish in the limestone soil, from mid-winter primroses to the cowslips and gentians of spring, while in summer Inisheer is ablaze with colour from purple cranesbill, white roses, honeysuckle, wild orchids, thyme, blue harebells, yellow centuary, and (in the neat gardens) hollyhocks, gladioli, and carnations. The song of the lark and the call of the cuckoo can be heard in high summer.

Here are built the currachs which are the traditional rowing boats in this part of the world. Originally the currach was made by stretching animal hide over a light wooden frame. It has the advantage of being easily carried ashore and needing no moorings. Today the currach is built of wood brought over from the mainland and imported canvas instead of the animal hide, the canvas being waterproofed with a coat of tar. The normal crew for a currach is three men, and for long trips these days they sometimes use an outboard motor. An Aran currach should not carry more than eight persons.

Inisheer has a communal hall where they hold *ceilidhs* – Irish dances to the music of an accordion. The proceedings are of course enlivened with songs, visitors being asked to contribute solos.

The islander women make the traditional woven belt of the islands, the *cris*, as well as the Aran sweaters which are knitted from memory, without any written instructions. You will see donkeys and ponies on Inisheer, but never a car (there are no roads to take them), and the only discordant noise is that of the island's two tractors.

Accommodation: there are various islanders who take in

visitors, and even when one arrives unexpectedly one will be told, 'The island's packed out but nobody's ever been left stuck yet.' There is one public house.

Roman Catholic Church.

INISHERK

SITUATION: in Kilkieran Bay, County Galway, close to Furnace Island and $1\frac{1}{2}$ miles off the mainland.
AREA: 71 acres.
POPULATION: 28.
ACCESS: by boat from Kilkieran.

The island has good fishing.

INISHFREE

SITUATION: $\frac{3}{4}$ mile w. of Carnboy Point, County Donegal.
AREA: 1 mile by $1\frac{1}{4}$ miles.
ACCESS: by boat from the mainland, but navigation is hazardous as the island is fringed by a bank of rocks extending 6 cables SE. from its SE. end and some of these are under water.

Inishfree is one of the Aranmore Isles (q.v.).

INISHGLORA

SITUATION: 3 miles w. of the Mullet Peninsula, County Mayo.
AREA: 50 acres.
POPULATION: uninhabited.
ACCESS: by boat from the mainland.

There has been some argument as to the origin of this island's name. It is also spelt Inishgluaire. Taken literally, its interpretation from the Gaelic means 'island of brightness', which is probably the true meaning. There are some who claim it means 'island of the voice', and others who say that *glora* is a corruption of *gloria*, giving the meaning 'island of glory'.

It is the chief of a small group of islets which mainly come under the heading of rocks. They are all easily distinguishable from a distance because of the permanent white froth of the sea which ebbs and flows around them.

St Brendan founded a monastery here in the 6th century and its remains, including three oratories, three stone-built cells, and a number of cross-incised stones, are enclosed by a ruined cashel wall. According to the *Book of Ballmote*, written about the year 1400, 'on Inis Gluair in Irrus Downan, the bodies thither brought do not rot, but their nails and hairs grow and everyone recognises his father and grandfather for a long time after death; and no meat will putrefy on it even without being salted.'

Book: *Notes on Irish Architecture*, by Lord Dunraven, 1875–7, vol. 1, page 40.

INISHGLUAIRE: *see* Inishglora.

INISHGORT: *see under* Westport Bay Islands.

THE INISHKEAS

SITUATION: 4 miles W. of the Belmullet Peninsula, County Mayo.
AREA: Inishkea North is 552 acres. Inishkea South is 388 acres.
POPULATION: uninhabited.
ACCESS: by boat from Fallmore, Belmullet Peninsula (6 miles).

These two islands, separated by less than a quarter of a mile, were inhabited up to 1931. They have the reputation of being in an area excellent for deep sea angling, which is perhaps the reason why the inhabitants were so unwilling to leave when pressed to do so by the Irish Free State Government.

On Inishkea North, on the S. side of the island near the now deserted village by the landing place, is Bailey Mor, a huge mound 500 ft wide and 60 ft high. S. of it there is a shell mound. Nearby a prehistoric dye workshop was found where purple dye was made from shell-fish.

In the early part of the century a whale fishery was established here by the Norwegians. At that time the population of the islands was 212. Each island had its own 'King'.

INISHLOE: *see under* Shannon River Islands.

Inishkea North, showing the ruins of the village which was abandoned in 1931 (Daphne Pochin Mould)

INISHMAAN

SITUATION: one of the Aran Islands, 1 mile SE. of Inishmore and 1 mile NW. of Inisheer, 30 miles SW. of Galway.

AREA: $3\frac{1}{2}$ sq. miles.

POPULATION: 420.

ACCESS: by air to Inishmore and thence by boat, or by boat from Galway by special arrangement.

There are two interesting ancient forts on Inishmaan

(one of the Aran Islands (q.v.)) – Dun Moher and Dun Conor. The last-named has been well restored and has an unusual construction, being oval in shape, more than 200 ft long and more than 100 ft wide. The trip by currach to Inishmaan from Inishmore (q.v.) is well worth while if only to examine these forts. There are also remains of ancient dwellings of a rectangular shape, but these are certainly of a much later date than either of the forts.

The inhabitants raise cattle and pigs and ship them across to Galway for selling. This is no easy feat as Inishmaan has no harbour, and the animals have to be transported by currach from a strand of the beach out to where the inter-island steamer is anchored. The women occupy themselves with weaving and spinning after they have washed and dried the fleeces from the shorn sheep.

In the middle Inishmaan rises to almost 300 ft, and then slopes gently to the S. It has three roads running S. to the centre of the island where they link with an E.–W. road. Most of the houses are built along the latter road.

The Church of the Seven Sons of the King lies close to the fort, Dun Conor, but it is badly ruined. Of greater interest is the Church of the Fairheaded One on the E. side of the island. O'Donovan, the celebrated Irish antiquarian, has said that it is 'the most perfect primitive Irish church in existence'. It is built of cyclopean stones, and has a square-headed doorway and narrow lancet-light.

Other sites of interest are the Bed of the Redhead, a small oblong enclosure with a stone cross at the E. end, and St Chínndheirg's Well, a freshwater spring said to have curative properties. During the religious 'Stations' held twice a year on Inishmaan

76

it is customary to visit the well, say certain prayers, and drink three times of its waters, a conch-like shell being kept there for this purpose.

Accommodation: there is a 10-bedroomed boarding-house on the island.

INISHMACOWNEY: *see under* Shannon River Islands.

INISHMEANE: *see* Inishsirrer and Inishmeane.

INISHMORE

SITUATION: the largest of the Aran Islands, 30 miles sw. of Galway.
AREA: 12 sq. miles.
POPULATION: 1,779.
ACCESS: by the 'Islander' air service from Galway, or by boat.

This is an island of memories of the distant pagan past, of the early Christians who created what was in effect one of the first universities in the Western World, of invasion by Cromwell's forces and, not least, of former inhabitants to whom various stone monuments have been erected alongside the roads. It is an island that has entranced and inspired many men of letters from the melancholic J. M. Synge to Liam O'Flaherty, whose stories of the life of the Aran Islands (q.v.) have found a niche in literature.

Rising to 460 ft at its highest point, Inishmore has a long range of cliffs of geological interest on its W. coast. The principal village is Kilronan, at the quay of which the island steamer calls – a settlement of about 250 people, with shops, hotel, and post office. About 1 mile distant in the same bay is the village of Killeany, in the vicinity of which are some of the best antiquities on the island. Here is St Enda's Church, and on a hill nearby the remains of a round tower, while slightly to the W. is the ruin of Teampul Bennan (St Brennan's Church), which is one of the earliest Irish churches, measuring only $10\frac{3}{4}$ ft long by 7 ft wide. It probably dates from the 7th century, possibly earlier. The gables are high and at an acute angle, while the entrance is so narrow that the top of the doorway is only $1\frac{3}{4}$ ft wide.

Near the church are the remains of stone-roofed huts. But there is much more of interest on the way from Killeany, going NW. to Kilmurvey. One passes other early churches such as St Kieran's, one of a group in this area known as the 'Seven Churches', and including Teampul a Phoill, Teampul Mac Duagh and Teampul Brecain. The principal church of this group is Teampul Brecain. It is not as old as Teampul Bennan, but is remarkable for its graveyard, which contains many early inscribed stones, including one with the inscription 'VII Romani'. Another of the churches has the romantic title of 'Church of the Four Comely Saints'.

To see this extensive evidence of the Christian faith on the island is to lift the curtain on what must have been the first seat of learning in this part of the world, an outpost which kept alive the torch of knowledge and civilisation in the Dark Ages. Classical culture and Christianity were both preserved here

78

on Inishmore, and the torch must have been carried out to many distant places by missionaries from Inishmore.

Close by the 'Seven Churches' is a small space enclosed by a wall only 18 in high, known as 'The Bed of the Holy Ghost'. Pilgrims have come here from time immemorial to seek cures for a variety of illnesses. The chief treatment is said to be to sleep in the open space for three Saturday nights between the Feast of St Peter and St Paul and St MacDara's Day. Those who sleep here borrow blankets from nearby cottages. Set against the wall is a small, crude cross, the shaft of which is carved ornamentally with a scene of the Crucifixion.

Inishmore's inhabitants are superstitious as well as being intensely religious. Some boys up to the age of eight wear skirts, and the reason given for this is that the people believe in fairies. The boys are dressed in skirts so that they will not be carried off by the fairies. For it is always said that fairies steal only little boys, and that to disguise the boys from the fairies they must be dressed as girls.

On the s. coast of Inishmore is Dun Aengus, the remains of an ancient fort, which has attracted the attention not merely of archaeologists but of many modern architects. It has a triple line of ramparts on a projection of the cliff. Its whole area must at one time have occupied something like 30 acres, the middle and inner lines of the defensive network being horseshoe-shaped. Dun Aengus has been described as 'the most magnificent barbaric monument now extant in Europe'. All the defences of the fort are on rising ground and, with a sheer cliff as its boundary, it must have been almost impregnable in its hey-day (1st century AD).

79

G

Dun Aengus Fort on Inishmore (Irish Tourist Board)

There are other forts on the island – Dun Onaght, a circular fort which is a short distance NW. of Kilmurvey, Dun Oghill and Dhu Caher.

Accommodation: there are hotels on Inishmore both at Kilronan and Kilmurvey. Some cottagers also take visitors. Public houses.

Book: *The Islands of Ireland*, by Thomas H. Mason, Mercier Press, Cork, rev. edn. 1967.

INISHMURRAY

SITUATION: 6 miles NW. of Grange, County Sligo.
AREA: 209 acres.
POPULATION: 79 (possibly seasonal figure).
ACCESS: by hired boat from Grange or Streedagh.

Like many other islands off this w. coast of Ireland, Inishmurray has slowly been denuded of its greenery by the cutting away of turf for fuel from the rocky surface.

The island has no cliffs and is low-lying, so much so in fact that one dark night in World War II a destroyer captain mistook it for a German submarine and fired a torpedo, which did no damage but scared the inhabitants out of their beds. In those days there were more than a hundred people living on the island, eking out a somewhat solitary existence with no roads, no church, no inn, and not even a shop.

The Vikings came to Inishmurray about 800 AD, but before this Celtic missionaries had visited the isle and left their mark there. It is said that St Columcille, wishing to make amends for some sin he had committed, went to Inishmurray and voluntarily put himself under the discipline of a priest named Molaise, later to become the island's patron saint. St Columcille is reputed to have been something of a woman-hater and because of this, legend has it, men and women were always buried in separate graveyards on Inishmurray.

The most interesting feature of the island is its wealth of Christian antiquities, most of which are enclosed in a circular space surrounded by a wall of

Inishmurray, County Sligo, showing the remains of the huge stone fort and ancient church (Daphne Pochin Mould)

loose stones. The probability is that this enclosure dates back to pre-Christian times and that the monastery created by St Molaise in the 6th century was built out of the remains of a pagan fort.

Within the circular space, the wall of which was restored in 1880, are the remains of three oratories, two altars, and two beehive cells used by hermit monks, as well as various stone pillars and inscribed stones. The men's cemetery is inside the enclosed space, the women's cemetery being some distance outside it.

In Teach Molaise, as one of the small oratories is called, is a wooden statue beside the altar. Local opinion is that it is a statue of St Molaise, but as experts have pointed out the statue is similar to some of the 16th century, and it may originally have been part of a figurehead from a wrecked Spanish galleon at the time of the Armada.

Some of the inscriptions on the stones are in a mixture of Gaelic and Latin. Other notable features on the island are two 'holy wells' and a curious beehive cell which is referred to as the 'Bath House'. Apparently it was used as a cure for rheumatism, the patient sweating it out inside the cell close up against the heat from a pile of burning peat ashes. In principle it would seem to be similar in function to a Turkish bath.

Despite the association with St Molaise, Inishmurray takes its name from Muiredeach, the patron saint of the diocese of Killala, and one of the gravestones bears the inscription: 'A prayer for Muiredeach Ua Comocain. He sleeps here.'

The most substantial building on the island is the Inishmurray National School, built in 1899, with its slate roof and broken school desks still in the main classroom. It is said that one of the main reasons for the departure of Inishmurray's inhabitants was that too close a watch had been kept on their illicit making of *poteen*. But it is a tragedy that so little has been done to preserve the antiquities of the island, and the restoration work done as far back as 1880 by the Office of Public Works is still much criticised.

The Inishmurray 'cursing stones' – five special stones inscribed with patterns, known as the *Clocha Breaca* – have traditionally been used to bring down maledictions on one's enemies. The *Shell Guide to Ireland* records a visit to Inishmurray by an Englishwoman during the last war to 'turn the stones against Hitler'.

Books: *The Islands of Ireland*, by Thomas H. Mason, Mercier Press, Cork, rev. edn. 1967; *Shell Guide to Ireland*, by Lord Killanin and Michael V. Duignan, rev. edn. 1972.

INISHMUSKERRY

SITUATION: lying close to Mweenish Island, County Galway.
AREA: 6 acres.
POPULATION: uninhabited.
ACCESS: by boat from Ard.

INISHNABRO: *see under* Blaskets, the.

INISHOO: *see under* Westport Bay Islands.

INISHSIRRER AND INISHMEANE

SITUATION: $\frac{1}{2}$ to 1 mile W. of the Gweedore Peninsula, County Donegal, and 1 mile N. of Gola Island.
AREA: 240 acres.
POPULATION: uninhabited.
ACCESS: by boat from Bunbeg in good weather.

Only a few miles S. of the bleak Bloody Foreland of NW. Donegal, these two islands are the most northerly of the group that lies in Gweedore Bay. Similar to

Gola, they are both bleak and rocky, and have recently been abandoned by the tiny fishing communities who occupied them.

Inishsirrer is slightly the larger island and is noted as a good area for lobster fishing.

INISHTOOSKERT

SITUATION: one of the Blaskets, 6 miles SW. of Slea Head, County Kerry.
AREA: 85 acres.
POPULATION: uninhabited.
ACCESS: by boat from Dunquin.

'A reptilian monster, dark and threatening, with its jagged silhouette against the sky and its body in shadow straddling the ocean' is how Thomas Mason describes Inishtooskert in his book *The Islands of Ireland*.

It is not far from Great Blasket, the principal island in the Blaskets (q.v.), and is inhabited by a wide variety of sea birds.

INISHTRAVIN

SITUATION: 2 miles E. of Kilkieran Pier and 1 mile SW. of Garrivinnagh in County Galway.
AREA: 192 acres.
POPULATION: 93.
ACCESS: by boat from Kilkieran Pier.

Inishtravin has a narrow waist of land which connects its E. and W. ends, and is surrounded by a number of tiny islets on the N. and W. Perhaps from the explorer's point of view the main attraction in this area is not so much Inishtravin itself as the uninhabited miniature islands which beckon the picnicker and adventurer in search of solitude.

There is a tiny settlement with a school on the island.

INISHTURK

SITUATION: 4 miles NE. of Inishbofin and 7 miles W. of Cross Lough, County Galway.
AREA: 136 acres.
POPULATION: 120.
ACCESS: by boat from Inishbofin or the mainland.

Inishturk means 'The Island of the Boar'. It is composed of Ordovician slates which run across the island in ribs and hollows, giving it the curious appearance of a ridged galvanised iron roof. There are some fine cliffs on the W.

There is a sheltered haven where boats can land, and good fishing in the vicinity. The story is told locally of how the Irish rounded up the last two Danes on this island, a father and son who possessed the secret for making heather ale. Neither would reveal the recipe, so both were thrown over the cliffs into the sea.

See also Caher.

INISHVICKILLANE

SITUATION: one of the Blaskets, 8 miles off Slea Head,
    County Kerry.
AREA: 199 acres.
POPULATION: uninhabited.
ACCESS: by boat from Dunquin.

The most southerly of the Blaskets (q.v.), Inishvickillane is about 3 miles SW. of Great Blasket (q.v.),
and is reputed to have received five survivors from
the Spanish Armada, who drew lots for the privilege
of marrying the only single woman on the island.
The disappointed four are then said to have sailed
off to the mainland in a currach.

INNISCOO: *see under* Aranmore Isles.

INNISKERAGH: *see under* Aranmore Isles.

IOCHTAR: *see under* Aranmore Isles.

IRELAND'S EYE

SITUATION: 1 mile N. of the Howth Peninsula, Dublin
    Bay.
AREA: $\frac{1}{2}$ mile by $\frac{1}{2}$ mile.
POPULATION: nil, except seasonally.
ACCESS: by boat from Howth. Group arrangements may
    be made with Irish Sea Anglers, Bayside, Sutton,
    County Dublin.

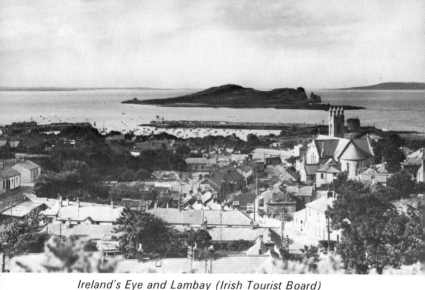

Ireland's Eye and Lambay (Irish Tourist Board)

A tiny islet, much favoured by holiday-makers from Dublin in quest of a day's outing, though its only real object of interest is the remains of one of the early Christian chapels. Like Dalkey it was once a monastic settlement.

ISLAND CRONE: *see under* Aranmore Isles.

JACKDAW ISLAND: *see under* Strangford Lough Islands.

JANE'S ROCK: *see under* Strangford Lough Islands.

KEDGE: *see under* Roaringwater Bay Isles.

KENMARE RIVER ISLANDS

SITUATION: in the broad estuary and lower reaches of the Kenmare River between Lamb's Head and Kenmare.
POPULATION: uninhabited.
ACCESS: by boat from Parknasilla or Kenmare.

The islands of the Kenmare River are tiny, but fascinatingly beautiful and, as they are spread out from Lamb's Head right up to Kenmare, some 27 miles distant, they are accessible from various points along the river, which in this area is about 3–4 miles wide.

Some of the islets would make admirable summer holiday homes for the discerning. Close to Parknasilla the river is dotted with wooded islets, some with rustic bridges and shady walks. There must be at least a score of islets, some almost too minute to mention.

Particularly worthy of mention are Garinish (Kerry) (q.v.), Abbey Island (q.v.), Rossdohan (which has tropical shrubs and faces Derryguin Castle), Ormonde's Island, Rossmore (off Coongar Harbour), Greenan and the Dunkerrons (q.v.), and Dinish Island (Kerry).

LAMBAY

SITUATION: 4 miles W. of County Dublin and 16 miles NE. of the city of Dublin.
AREA: 2 miles by 1 mile.
POPULATION: 15.
ACCESS: by boat from Portrane or Rush, but permission to land must be obtained first.

As its name indicates, Lambay was first inhabited in historical times when the Viking raiders landed here in 795. When harbour works were carried out some few years ago examples of Neolithic and Bronze Age tools dating from 3000 to 500 BC were excavated, on the raised beach at the W. end of the island. Lambay still offers great scope to the archaeologist: dozens of flaked flints can be found here, sometimes in the rabbit warrens at the N. end of Lambay.

The rocks of Lambay are mainly of volcanic origin, quite distinct from the carboniferous limestone of the mainland. The cliffs are tall, and seals can be found gambolling at their feet, while all kinds of seabirds nest here. The island has been in the possession of Lord Revelstoke and his family for many years, and a former Lord Revelstoke built an imposing mansion here. Lambay is today a sanctuary for wild life. The peregrine falcon, raven and shearwater – especially the Manx shearwater – all nest on the island.

St Columcille is said to have founded a monastery here, but no trace of this survives today, though Trinity Well, in the centre of the island close to Knockbane (418 ft), may be a relic of this period. At

Lambay Island, County Dublin (Irish Tourist Board)

one time Lambay was used for the internment of Jacobite prisoners-of-war.

Of special note are the Garden Fort on Gouge Point, NE. of the small harbour, and Lambay Castle, the Revelstoke house designed by Sir Edwin Lutyens, who cleverly included in his design the remains of a small 15th-century castle formerly occupied by Archbishop Ussher (1581–1656).

LETTERMORE

SITUATION: 1 mile w. of the mainland of County Galway and 2 miles from Bealadangan.

AREA: $3\frac{1}{2}$ sq. miles.
POPULATION: 801.
ACCESS: by road and causeway link across Annaghvaan
Island to Bealadangan.

Lettermore lies in a sheltered position, close to the mainland of Galway on the E. side, with Kilkieran Bay and the headland of Ardmore Point, also on the mainland, to the W., Inishtravin Island (q.v.) to the N. and Gorumna (q.v.) to the S. It is linked to the mainland by a road which runs from Bealadangan by bridge to Annaghvaan (q.v.) and thence by causeway to Lettermore. Thence it continues across to Gorumna and from there by bridge over to the island of Lettermullen (q.v.).

There is a hill (364 ft) on the NW. of the island, and settlements at Creenagh on the NE., opposite Annaghvaan, and Lettermore on the S., facing Gorumna. At the latter there is also a school.

LETTERMULLEN

SITUATION: close to Gorumna Island and 4 miles SE. of
Ardmore Point, County Galway.
AREA: $1\frac{1}{4}$ sq. miles.
POPULATION: 460.
ACCESS: by road bridge from Gorumna, which is linked
by road, bridge, and causeway to the mainland at
Bealadangan.

Lettermullen marks the terminus of a road which runs from Bealadangan on the mainland, across the islands of Annaghvaan (q.v.), Lettermore (q.v.), and Gorumna (q.v.) to the E. side of Lettermullen. It has one tiny settlement with a school, and a small hill (121 ft) in the SE. corner.

Like Lettermore to the N., Lettermullen is surrounded by tiny islands on the N. and W. It is in fact a splendid stepping-off place for the explorer of tiny, uninhabited islands rarely marked on maps. If one has a boat they are easy to explore in a single day, as they are all huddled together within a few hundred yards of one another, and in some cases much less. Indeed, seen from a high-flying aircraft, these islets are so densely packed that they appear as one mass with Lettermullen as the centre.

The author counted no fewer than ten islets around Lettermullen, but one of these, Dog Island, on the S., is so low-lying as to be barely discernible except when one is quite close to it. The highest is Golam Head off the SW. extremity of Lettermullen, distinguishable by a square tower on a high rock above the sea.

See also Dinish (Galway) and Furnace Island.

Accommodation: the best place to stay for exploring this area is not on Lettermullen, but at the inn on Gorumna, just across the bridge from Lettermullen.

LIGHTHOUSE ISLAND

SITUATION: $2\frac{1}{2}$ miles NE. of the coastguard station, Groomsport Harbour, County Down.
AREA: 60 acres.
POPULATION: 3.

ACCESS: by boat from Donaghadee, by arrangement with Mr D. W. D. Leroux, 56 Warren Road, Donaghadee.

This is one of the Copeland Islands (q.v.) and is the site of the Copeland Bird Observatory, owned by the National Trust and containing the only ringing station in Northern Ireland. About two-thirds of the area is suitable for grazing land. Though it is called Lighthouse Island, there is no longer a lighthouse here.

LITTLE SALTEE: *see under* Saltee Islands.

LITTLE SKELLIG: *see under* Skelligs, the.

LONG ISLAND (Antrim): *see under* Skerry Islands (Antrim).

LONG ISLAND (Cork)

SITUATION: in Roaringwater Bay, County Cork, 1 mile S. of the mainland and lying at the SW. end of the bay.
AREA: 2 miles by $\frac{1}{4}$ mile.
POPULATION: 47.
ACCESS: by boat from the mainland.

This long, narrow-waisted isle rises to 97 ft near its centre and slopes to Copper Point, its low, shelving NE. extremity, where stands a 45 ft high stone beacon. Duff Point, its SW. extremity, is named after Duff

Island near by. It has two piers, on the N. and NW. of the island.

See also Roaringwater Bay Isles.

LONG ISLAND (Down): *see under* Strangford Lough Islands.

LYTHE ROCK: *see under* Strangford Lough Islands.

MAHAREE ISLANDS

SITUATION: 1 to $2\frac{1}{2}$ miles N. of Rough Point, at the NW. end of Tralee Bay, County Kerry.
TOTAL AREA: 25 acres.
POPULATION: uninhabited.
ACCESS: by boat from the village of Fahamore.

A group of tiny islets, the Maharees are of interest because of their remains of an anchoritic monastery. The largest of the isles is Illauntannig, 1 mile N. of Rough Point. Its name is a corruption of *Oilean tSeanaigh*, meaning 'The Island of St Seanach', who was closely associated with St Seanan of Scattery Island.

St Seanach founded a monastery here in the 6th century and its remains are today enclosed by a massive drystone cashel. There are also the remains of a tiny church, three burial monuments, and some incised crosses. On the other major island, Illaunimmil, are a prehistoric chambered tomb and a stone circle.

95

Maharee, County Kerry (Irish Tourist Board)

MAHEE

SITUATION: on the w. side of Strangford Lough, County
Down, $\frac{3}{4}$ mile from the shore.
AREA: 176 acres.
POPULATION: 13.
ACCESS: by boat from Ardmillan.

Mahee is also known as Bird Island. It is the largest
of the many islands in Strangford Lough (q.v.), and
is owned by Mr P. P. Mackie. By arrangement with

the National Trust it is scheduled as a winter refuge for birds and manned by NT wardens.

It is a delightfully wooded isle, extremely beautiful in summer when it is visited by flocks of tern. Centuries ago the monks of Nendrum made an early Christian settlement on Mahee.

MANNIN ISLAND: *see under* Roaringwater Bay Isles.

MEW ISLAND

SITUATION: one of the Copeland Islands, lying close to the E. side of Lighthouse Island, $2\frac{1}{2}$ miles NE. of the coastguard station, Groomsport Harbour, County Down.
AREA: 26 acres.
POPULATION: 2.
ACCESS: by boat from Groomsport or Donaghadee.

The smallest of the Copeland Islands (q.v.), Mew is the one which today possesses the lighthouse – 121 ft above sea level, with one of the most powerful lanterns in the world, acting as a guide to the entrance to Belfast Lough. Each minute the lantern gives out four short white flashes, and in foggy weather a diaphone gives four short blasts every half minute. Terns and sea-swallows breed on Mew Island.

MIDDLE CALF: *see under* Roaringwater Bay Isles.

MIDDLE ISLAND: *see under* Garvan Isles.

MOYNISH MORE: *see under* Westport Bay Islands.

THE MULLET ISLANDS

SITUATION: extending from Broadhaven in the N. to Blacksod Bay, County Mayo, and the area around Achill Island in the S.

TOTAL AREA: $2\frac{3}{4}$ sq. miles.

POPULATION: uninhabited.

ACCESS: by boat from most points on the Mullet Peninsula, from which they take their name.

This corner of Ireland has many islands ranging from Achill (q.v.), the largest island off the Irish coast, Achillbeg (q.v.), and the Inishkeas (q.v.) to several tiny islets, often little more than plant-covered sandbanks, along the southerly arm of Broadhaven.

They are all relatively easy to explore on one trip as a short canal has been cut to give passage between Broadhaven and Blacksod Bay. The whole of the Mullet is a charming, if somewhat desolate and treeless area, full of creeks and miniature islands, some of them bearing traces of the anchorite priests of the early Christian Church.

MUTTON ISLAND (Clare)

SITUATION: $2\frac{1}{2}$ miles W. of Quilty, County Clare.
AREA: 185 acres.
POPULATION: 20.
ACCESS: by boat from Tromro Point, near Quilty, but there is no specially recorded landing place.

Mutton Island is the largest of a group of three islands off the Clare coast at Tromro Point. It lies off Doughmore shoals, rises to 101 ft, and is fringed with foul ground. The ruined tower of an old church associated with the name of St Senan stands on its W. side. There is also a small cemetery where the island's dead of all ages are buried.

Seven families lived on Mutton within living memory and names such as Kelleher, Gallagher, and Griffin were familiarly associated with the island, which is part of the parish of Kilmurry-Ibrickane. As its name suggests, much of Mutton is good pasture land, and there is a lake some 3–4 acres in size which has been known to offer scope for fishing.

A Mr Stacpoole owned the island throughout most of the 19th century. It then passed into the hands of a Mr McDonough, who later disposed of it to an Ennis victualler, Mr J. Griffey.

On the E. side Mutton is nearly connected to a stony barrier which at low water dries out and extends about $4\frac{1}{2}$ cables NNW. from Lurga Point, on the mainland. At the N. extremity of the barrier is Craggaun Rock, which dries about 7 ft, and between it and Mutton Island is a narrow passage with a depth of 3 ft.

Books: *History of Kilmurry-Ibrickane*, by Archdeacon P. Ryan, Clare Champion Ltd, 1969; *see also* book review section of *North Munster Journal*, vol. 12 (1969).

MUTTON ISLAND
(Galway)

SITUATION: in Galway Bay, lying off the approaches to Galway Harbour.
AREA: 1 mile by $\frac{1}{4}$ mile.
POPULATION: uninhabited.
ACCESS: at low water across a stony spit by which the island is connected to the mainland; otherwise by boat.

This is a low, rocky islet, lying on an extensive rocky flat (a considerable part of which dries out at low water) extending $\frac{1}{2}$ mile w. from the lighthouse. The island protects Galway Harbour from westerly winds.

MWEENISH

SITUATION: 3 miles S. of Carna and 14 miles SE. of Clifden, County Galway.
AREA: 613 acres.
POPULATION: 376.
ACCESS: it is connected to the mainland by a bridge.

As Mweenish has the atmosphere of a real island, it is included in this book even though its bridge link to the mainland should technically rule it out. The sandy beaches are splendid, and there is much to see, notably the Marine Biology Station.

It is an ideal island to ramble around, with much beautiful scenery and, surprisingly, quite a lot of activity. Mweenish, with its forty houses, is the centre of an interesting community experiment. Up to about four years ago it was self-contained community, doing its own weaving, carpeting, blacksmith's work, and boat-making. Then Gael Linn distributed a number of motor-boats for lobster fishing, and the catch was sold back to Gael Linn for processing at the factory at Ard. The cost of the boats was deducted. The factory, which has been handed over to a local fishermen's co-operative, is equipped with refrigeration rooms, and part of it is now used for metal work.

At present there are five 25-ft motor-boats and numerous currachs on the island and they land at Portach Pier, which was improved a few years ago. Fishing boats of up to 30 ft are built on Mweenish, which at one time was one of the foremost boat-building centres in Ireland. It is intended to introduce a new boat-building project on the island and also to lay a slip-way. Weaving is still done in Mweenish.

See also Duck Island, Inishmuskerry.

Accommodation: apply to the Western Regional Tourist Organisation Ltd, Ireland West House, Galway.

OMEY

SITUATION: close inshore to the Cleggan Peninsula in County Galway.
AREA: 534 acres.
POPULATION: 101.
ACCESS: at low tide on foot across the $1\frac{1}{2}$ mile strand then linking the island to the mainland.

Omey Island is noted for its horse, cycle, and currach races, held there annually. They draw crowds from far and wide, from Dublin débutantes as well as from the peasantry.

The sandhills overlooking the hard, long, sandy beach make a natural grandstand for the events. They are decked out with stalls selling drinks, tea, and food.

The currach races depend upon the state of the sea. Jockeys in the horse races are mostly small boys under the age of fifteen.

ORMONDE'S ISLAND: *see under* Kenmare River Islands.

OWEY

SITUATION: $3\frac{1}{4}$ miles WNW. of Rosses Bay, County Donegal, separated from Cruit Island by Owey Sound.
AREA: 306 acres.

POPULATION: 152.
ACCESS: by boat from Cruit Island.

This island rises to a height of 329 ft, and its main interest is its bird life. Access is from Cruit Island, but it should be explained that Cruit is not an island as defined in this book, but is linked to the mainland by a road from Dungloe.

PARTON: *see under* Strangford Lough Islands.

PEGGY'S ISLAND: *see under* Strangford Lough Islands.

PIG ISLAND (Down): *see under* Strangford Lough Islands.

PIG ISLAND (Mayo)

SITUATION: close inshore to Porturlin, near to Portacloy, County Mayo.
AREA: 8 acres.
POPULATION: uninhabited.
ACCESS: by boat from Porturlin.

PUFFIN ISLAND (Kerry)

SITUATION: less than 1 mile W. of the SW. tip of County
   Kerry, and 3 miles SSW. of Portmagee.
AREA: 45 acres.
POPULATION: uninhabited.
ACCESS: by boat from the mainland.

A wild, rocky island interesting only for its bird life.

RATHLIN

SITUATION: 7 miles N. of Ballycastle, County Antrim,
   and 18 miles W. of the Mull of Kintyre, Scotland.
AREA: $5\frac{1}{3}$ sq. miles.
POPULATION: 351.
ACCESS: by boat from Ballycastle.

Generally known as Rathlin, this island's correct
name is Raghery or Rechra. It is as much, if not
more, a part of Scottish mythology and history as it
is of Irish. 'When one stands at the North-East
corner of the island,' writes Thomas H. Mason,

it is hard to realise that one is in Ireland, the Scottish
coast appearing almost as near as the mainland of Ireland;
and indeed one realises when speaking to the islanders
that they are even more Scottish than Irish. Their accent
is a cross between Northern Irish and Lowland Scots.
They enlist in the Scottish regiments and there is much
coming and going between both mainlands. This inter-

Rathlin Island, off Northern Ireland: refuge of Robert Bruce (J. Allan Cash)

change follows the prehistoric movements, as there is no doubt that the first settlers came to Ireland via the narrow sea of the North Channel, and later raids and plantations were carried out by distant kinsmen of the earlier inhabitants.

There is a motor-boat service to Rathlin from Ballycastle, and it provides something of a thrill as it races through the turbulent stretch of sea known as the *Brochan*, or 'boiling porridge pot'. For those using sail the *Brochan* can be a severe test. The very bold attempt surf-riding in the vicinity.

Most of the inhabitants are engaged in farming and fishing, and the main settlement is at Church Bay on the s. side of the L-shaped island, where the chief landing place is also sited. Close by is the manor house which used to be one of the homes of the Viscounts Gage. In the interior are two lakes which are full of fish, and a quite surprising variety of scenery. Rathlin has much of interest to the fisherman, bird-watcher, botanist, and archaeologist. It also offers many pleasant walks, from the verdant interior to the cliffs of the SE. extremity, where there is a formation of rock resembling that of the Giant's Causeway on the mainland nearby – a volcanic formation producing a mixture of limestone and basalt which caused Charles Kingsley in *Westward Ho!* to compare Rathlin's alternate black and white cliffs to 'a drowned magpie'.

The cliffs are occupied by a wide range of bird life from the guillemot and kittiwake to the razorbill and puffin. The prevalence of flint on the island is a reminder that a flourishing Neolithic industry existed here: archaeologists have established that flint implements were actually exported from Rathlin in the Late Stone Age. The island was known to both Pliny and Ptolemy, and mentioned in their writings. Pliny designates Rathlin as 'Ricnia'.

Both St Columcille and St Comgall are said to have visited Rathlin, and it was the first part of Ireland to be invaded by the Vikings. It was here, too, that Robert Bruce, King of Scotland, sought refuge from the English in 1306. The basalt cave in which he hid is situated near the NE. corner of Rathlin in Ballycarry. It is around this cave that the legend of Bruce and the spider has been created. So impressed was he by the patience and tenacity of a spider in weaving its web that the lesson 'if you don't at first succeed, try, try again' was implanted in his mind. After this he returned to Scotland, triumphed over the English at Bannockburn, and was crowned King. Near the cave is also Bruce's Castle, something of a misnomer for a high headland defended by a crumbling wall on the landward side.

There are also some unusual caves worth exploring to the s. of Church Bay. At Doonmore on the N. coast is a stone ring-fort, and other interesting relics of the past are a 'sweat house' I mile NW. of Church Bay, and a circular enclosure, probably a relic of early Christian days.

Ulster, which has seen so many savage massacres both in ancient and modern times, has perhaps witnessed its worst butcheries on the island of Rathlin. The Campbells of Argyll were responsible for the first mass murder raid on the island, but the blackest mark set against any invader was in Elizabethan times. In 1597 the chieftains of Antrim, the MacDonnels, while engaged in fighting the English forces, dispatched the aged, the women and the children to Rathlin for safety. The English fleet sailed to the island and put almost every living person to death. For several years after this horrible massacre Rathlin was uninhabited.

Michael MacLaverty, who spent part of his boyhood on Rathlin, has become the best-known of the island's writers. In a number of his novels he has introduced Rathlin as a setting, while Olga Fielden (Mrs F. H. Lamond) in *Island Story* thinly disguised Rathlin as 'Rathnaheena'.

Accommodation: some is available in Church Bay.
Books: *Island Story*, by Olga Fielden, Jonathan Cape, 1933; *Call My Brother Back*, by Michael MacLaverty, Longmans, 1939; *The Game Cock and Other Stories*, by Michael MacLaverty, Jonathan Cape, 1949.

RATHLIN O'BIRNE

SITUATION: I mile W. of Loughen Point, the W. extremity of Malinbeg Head, which forms the entrance to Donegal Bay, County Donegal.
AREA: 30 acres.
POPULATION: 3.
ACCESS: by boat from Malin More.

This island is inhabited only by the maintenance team of its lighthouse. It rises to a height of 95 ft and exhibits a light to an elevation of 116 ft from a white tower on the W. side of the island. The lighthouse is equipped with radio telephone. A landing can only be effected in moderate weather on the SW. side of the lighthouse. On the W. side of the island are four rocky islets with steep sides.

REAGH ISLAND: *see under* Strangford Lough Islands.

RED ISLAND: *see under* Skerries (Dublin), the.

RINGAROGY

SITUATION: 5 miles SW. of Skibbereen in Roaringwater Bay, County Cork.
AREA: 950 acres.
POPULATION: 20. (1970).
ACCESS: by boat from Schull or Baltimore.

Scores of tiny islets lend enchantment to Roaringwater Bay, County Cork (Aerofilms)

ROARINGWATER BAY ISLES

SITUATION: in Roaringwater Bay, County Cork.
TOTAL AREA: approximately 53 sq. miles.
POPULATION: 1,105.
ACCESS: by boat from the mainland.

N. of Baltimore lies Roaringwater Bay which is

studded – indeed, in places almost choked – with islands of all shapes and sizes, large and small, occupied and uninhabited, and of these usually a few at least are on estate agents' books as being 'for sale'.

A curious feature of these isles is that many of them can find their counterparts in name if nothing else across the Atlantic in Long Island Sound. It should be noted that Roaringwater Bay is an extensive shallow inlet at the NE. corner of Long Island Bay, which may explain how the names came to be borrowed in the USA.

There is an archipelago of these isles right across the mouth of Roaringwater Bay. The largest of them are Castle Island (q.v.), Long Island (q.v.), and Hare. The last-named has a population of twenty. The other principal inhabited islands are Castle Island, Long Island, Ringarogy (q.v.), Inishbeg, and some of the tiny group known as the Spanish Isles.

Most of these islands offer delightful prospects for picnickers in search of solitude in summertime, and almost all are verdant and fertile. Several of them have fresh water.

Duff Island lies just S. of Long Island, $\frac{1}{2}$ mile E. of Goat Island, while Horse Island lies $\frac{1}{2}$ mile ENE. of Castle Island and close to West Skeam, the outermost of a group of isles close to the mainland. Mannin Island, which rises to 56 ft, lies $1\frac{3}{4}$ miles NE. of Horse Island in the inner part of the bay.

Other isles are Coney; the Garrilauns; West Calf, Middle Calf, and East Calf (the last two being steep on some sides and separated by a channel of water $3\frac{1}{2}$ cables wide between East Calf and Middle Calf); Carthy, which lies at the centre of the approach to Roaringwater Bay, close to Castle Island; Bininy, the most northerly of the group, 2 cables NE. of Carthy;

Birds' Island; Kedge; and Greens Island. Most of these are uninhabited, but Greens is occupied by wild goats and cattle.

ROEILLAUN: *see under* Westport Bay Islands.

ROSSDOHAN: *see under* Kenmare River Islands.

ROSSMORE: *see under* Kenmare River Islands.

ROUND ISLAND: *see under* Strangford Lough Islands.

RUTLAND

SITUATION: lies between Aran Island and Burtonport, County Donegal, $5\frac{1}{2}$ miles w. of Burtonport.
AREA: about 1 mile in circumference.
ACCESS: by boat from Burtonport.

A submarine cable connects Rutland Island, one of the Aranmore Isles (q.v.), to Burtonport. Rutland Harbour, which lies between Inishcoo and Rutland Island, is the chief anchorage in the North Sound of Aran. The Duke of Rutland, who gave his name to the island, attempted to create a port here in 1785, but he was thwarted by the Marquis of Conyngham, who developed Burtonport.

ST MACDARA'S ISLAND

SITUATION: 2 miles SW. of Ard, County Galway, and
  5 miles from Carna.
AREA: $\frac{1}{2}$ mile by $\frac{1}{2}$ mile.
POPULATION: uninhabited.
ACCESS: by boat from Ard.

A hillock of an island, facing the small harbour of
Ard, St MacDara's has been a place of pilgrimage
ever since St Sionnach MacDara founded a monastery
there in the 6th century. A pilgrimage takes place
every 16 July to the remains of the island's small
church, a minute partially-roofed oratory with a
high roof in the Celtic style. The pilgrimage is
followed by a regatta.

St MacDara's help is invoked against the perils of
the sea and, traditionally, boatmen passing the island
dip their sails three times in tribute to the saint. There
are pilgrimage stations, carved stones, and inscribed
slabs; most of the crosses are built of blue limestone
which was probably brought over from the mainland.
St MacDara's bed – so styled – is one of the relics
pointed out to visitors.

ST PATRICK'S ISLE (Dublin)

SITUATION: one of the Skerries group of islands off the

coast 19 miles N. of Dublin, $1\frac{1}{4}$ miles ENE. of Skerries Town.

AREA: 40 acres.
POPULATION: uninhabited.
ACCESS: by boat from Skerries Town.

St Patrick is said to have landed on this small island in the Skerries (q.v.) group when voyaging to Tara. One legend is that people from the mainland raided the island and stole St Patrick's goat. An early monastery on St Patrick's Isle suffered from Viking raids in 795, and the marauders carried off the Shrine of St DoChonna.

A synod was held on the island in 1148, when it was decided to send a spokesman to Rome to request palls for the first Irish archbishops. By the 13th century the monastery had become an Augustine priory, and it was transferred to Holmpatrick. The only remains on the island now are a few stones that indicate a tufa-roofed church.

Today the island is owned privately by Mr Butty Sugrue, an Irishman living in London. Some time ago the island came into the news when it was put up for sale and a group of 'Hippies' made a bid for it with a view to turning it into a 'group paradise'. They failed, and it was then that Mr Sugrue bought it for £25,000. In 1971 a newspaper report suggested that 'Irish rebels might make a £60,000 undercover bid for St Patrick's Isle . . . to be used as an arms dump giving the IRA a strategic base outside British and Irish control.' Nothing came of this, and at the time of going to press the island is still up for sale. It is locally known as 'Church Island'.

SALTEE ISLANDS

SITUATION: 5 miles S. of Kilmore Quay, County
  Wexford.
TOTAL AREA: 308 acres.
POPULATION: 3.
ACCESS: by hired boat from Kilmore Quay.

There are two islands in the group, Great Saltee and
Little Saltee, the latter about $\frac{1}{2}$ mile NE. of the former.
Great Saltee is about $1\frac{1}{2}$ miles long and from $\frac{1}{4}$ to $\frac{3}{4}$
mile in width, and at one time was farmed, but it is
many years now since it reverted to its wild state and
in consequence became an exceptionally fine natural
bird sanctuary.

Great Saltee lies on one of the main flight lines of
migratory birds, and in late spring and early summer
thousands of birds come here in transit or to breed,
including the shag, fulmar petrel, cormorant, kittiwake, lapwing, razorbill, guillemot, Manx shearwater,
swallow, waxwing, magpie, jackdaw, Sandwich tern,
shelduck, peregrine falcon, lark, wren, rock pigeon,
and many kinds of gull. The civic guards from the
mainland take a keen interest in seeing that there are
no breaches of the Wild Birds Protection Act.

Thomas H. Mason has written of the island:
On a fine day we made an approximate estimate of the
numbers of birds floating on the surface of the sea and it
came to 750,000. This was a conservative rough count
which we made by counting the numbers in a section and

Opposite: *The Saltee Islands, now a bird sanctuary, off the
coast of Wexford (Daphne Pochin Mould)*

multiplying it to give an estimate only of those birds which were on the sea on the south side of the island, and we took no account of the birds on land or on the sea surrounding the east, north and west sides. Since then the birds have increased enormously. Portions of the cliffs, and even the boulders projecting from the boulder clay which were formerly unfrequented, are now so congested with bird life that there is a site shortage for nesting purposes. Taking all these facts into consideration I believe that a fair estimate should now place the numbers at about two-and-a-half million or three million birds.

There seems to be no reason to dispute this claim today.

No harbour exists on Great Saltee, and when the wind is in the N. a landing is difficult. In good weather in summer the island is often a mass of wild flowers as well as birds, hyacinths being particularly prominent; there are also masses of campions, sea pinks, and unusual rock plants.

The owner of the islands is Mr Michael O'Neill, of Dalkey. He is now only a summer visitor to the Saltees, but when in residence he hoists his personal flag on his house on the hill. He calls himself 'Prince Michael I of the Saltees', and his limestone throne stands on the flank of a hill and bears his arms – a shield held by two mermaids, each of its quarters containing a different sort of bird. A nearby obelisk bears a plaque, carved with his profile, which explains that the throne was erected in memory of his mother, to whom he vowed when only ten years old that one day he would own the Saltees and become their first 'Prince'. He cautions his heirs that they can only become his royal successors by being garbed in the robes and crown of the islands (regalia which he bought when he had himself crowned). Finally, the inscription exhorts all children with ambitions to work hard to achieve them.

Books: *The Islands of Ireland*, by Thomas H. Mason, Mercier Press, Cork, rev. edn. 1967.

SANDY COVE

SITUATION: 3 miles SW. of Kinsale, County Cork.
AREA: 13 acres.
POPULATION: uninhabited.
ACCESS: by boat from the mainland, but conditions are

A tiny island with no buildings, but possessing a boat slip-way. It was offered for sale at £5,000 a few years ago.

SCARIFF AND DEENISH

SITUATION: $4\frac{1}{2}$ to 5 miles W. of Lamb's Head, County Kerry.
TOTAL AREA: 366 acres.
POPULATION: 7.
ACCESS: by boat from the mainland, but conditions are frequently difficult for landing.

Two isolated islands situated close together, Scariff and Deenish are forbidding and precipitous. Scariff rises to 829 ft. There is a chain of sharp and steep rocks known as Scariff Hedges extending for 2 cables along the w. side of Scariff.

SCARONY: *see under* Garvan Isles.

SCATTERY

SITUATION: in the estuary of the River Shannon, $1\frac{1}{2}$ miles s. of Kilrush in County Clare.
AREA: 186 acrcs.
POPULATION: 6 (1970).
ACCESS: by boat from Cappagh Pier, Kilrush. Transport may be arranged at the Town Hall, Kilrush.

This is the chief of the many islands in the Shannon River (q.v.) estuary. It has a lighthouse with resident keepers.

Rich in antiquaries, Scattery has been considered a sacred place in Irish history from the earliest times of Christianity, for it was here that St Senan, who died in 554, made his retreat and founded a monastery.

In the 9th century Scattery was plundered by the Vikings. There are traces of five early churches on the island, the remains of St Senan's monastery, fragments of Romanesque carving, and a Round Tower rising to 125 ft.

Book: *Journal of the Royal Society of Antiquaries of Ireland*, vol. 27 (1897).

SHANNON RIVER ISLANDS

SITUATION: in the River Shannon estuary, ranging from Kilrush to Limerick.
TOTAL AREA: approximately $9\frac{1}{2}$ sq. miles.
POPULATION: uninhabited.
ACCESS: by boat from Kilrush and various points on either bank of the Shannon Estuary. Several of the islands are conveniently close to Shannon airport.

The whole estuary is studded with islands, the largest of which is Scattery (q.v.) at the W. extremity of the group. The greatest concentration of islets is in the NE. corner of the estuary where it broadens out in the N. in the direction of Clarecastle.

Most of the uninhabited islands are used for grazing: they are nearly all covered with grass and some are extremely beautiful, especially on a sunny evening shortly before sunset.

Canon Island, 2 miles E. of Kiladysert, is at the time of writing inhabited by two families, and has a pier on its S. side. In 1966 there were three families on Coney Island (Clare) (q.v.). Inishloe is not thought to be inhabited at present, but Inishmacowney (commonly called Horse Island) is occupied by five families. It has three separate landing points, two small harbours, and a small natural landing place. The other principal island is Deer, which has no population and is now used solely for grazing.

SHEELAHS, The: *see under* Strangford Lough Islands.

SHEEP ISLAND
(Antrim)

SITUATION: $2\frac{1}{2}$ miles off Ballintoy, County Antrim.
AREA: 10 acres.
POPULATION: uninhabited.
ACCESS: by boat, but only in very calm weather.

This is the largest of a group of rocky islets off Ballintoy, and it is controlled by the National Trust as a bird sanctuary. The other islands, mostly known as the Camplie, are insignificant large rocks of little interest.

SHERKIN

SITUATION: close inshore to Baltimore, County Cork.
AREA: 2 sq. miles.
POPULATION: 80 (1970).
ACCESS: there is a ferry service daily all the year round, with extra services in summer. Return trips each day. Return fare 50p.

This is the largest of several islands lying in and around Roaringwater Bay. Because of its proximity to the mainland and its splendid beaches and good bathing facilities, it is popular for excursions from Cork and the neighbouring towns and attracts hundreds of tourists in the summer months.

Sherkin Island from the mainland (Irish Tourist Board)

Below: *Sherkin Island: view of the Friary (Daphne Pochin Mould)*

Sherkin is a delightful place in which to ramble, bathe, and picnic, with much natural beauty. Near the landing place are the ruins of the O'Driscoll Castle of Dunnalong. Close by are the remains of what must have been an extremely attractive Franciscan abbey, built in 1460 by the O'Driscolls. Both the castle and the abbey were destroyed in 1537. There are also several *gallauns* and stone crosses, and a penal altar.

Worthy of note is the island's curious small harbour known as Horseshoe Harbour.

Accommodation: a holiday adventure camp for young people is run in the summer by Mr Matt Murphy.

SHOAN ISLAND: *see under* Strangford Lough Islands.

SKELLIG MICHAEL: *see under* Skelligs, The.

THE SKELLIGS

SITUATION: 10 miles w. of Bolus Head, County Kerry.
TOTAL AREA: 25 acres.
POPULATION: 5.
ACCESS: normally by courtesy of the Commissioners of Irish Lights from Ballinskelligs, Waterville, or Valencia.

The Skelligs are two rocky islets: Skellig Michael,

the larger, and Little Skellig. They are inhabited solely by the men who work the lighthouse on Skellig Michael, and are normally only accessible by means of the relief vessel which serves the lighthousemen. Even then a landing is sometimes impossible and always difficult. Though there are three landing places on Skellig Michael, personnel often have to be hoisted by cable from the ship, and supplies are hoisted onto a platform cut out of the solid rock.

Little Skellig is one of the relatively few breeding grounds for gannets in the Irish islands. Skellig Michael is a huge precipitous rock rising to twin peaks, of 750 ft and 650 ft respectively. Between the peaks is the only flat ground on the island, known as Christ's Saddle.

The larger island was, appropriately, dedicated to St Michael, the patron saint of high places. It was the site of a monastery in the 6th century, said to have been founded by St Fionan, and certainly one of the very early Christian settlements that kept the faith alive in the Dark Ages. The monastic site contains several of the beehive type of monastic cell known as *clochans*, once inhabited by hermits who existed on sea-birds' eggs and goats' milk. The cells are situated on a ridge of rock more than 500 ft in height, and Thomas H. Mason has described them as 'the most western of Christ's fortresses in the ancient world'. But remote as they are, they were well built and are still intact, despite the fact that a church built much later with mortar is in a ruinous condition.

The Vikings raided the Skelligs in 823 and, angered at the lack of any booty, took captive one of the monks in revenge. But it would seem that the Christian spirit survived this test, as later a Norse king, Olaf, was actually baptised here.

The Skelligs: an aerial view

There are two small oratories on Skellig Michael, in one of which is a small stone altar. Behind it is the small cemetery of the monks, marked by crude crosses and stones with crosses cut into them.

On Little Skellig, in addition to the gannets, are fulmar and stormy petrel.

Ninth-century honeycomb cells on the Skelligs (British Tourist Authority)

THE SKERRIES (Dublin)

SITUATION: close offshore from Skerries Town, a small
  seaside resort 19 miles N. of Dublin and 4 miles SE. of
  Balbriggan, County Dublin.
TOTAL AREA: 80 acres.
ACCESS: by boat from Skerries Town.

These three tiny islands shelter the resort of Skerries from the E. winds. Chief of them is Red Island, on which there is a martello tower and a holiday camp with facilities for visitors. St Patrick's Isle (q.v.) is locally known as 'Church Island'.

SKERRY ISLANDS (Antrim)

SITUATION: 1–1½ miles N. of Portrush, County Antrim.
TOTAL AREA: 50 acres.
POPULATION: uninhabited.
ACCESS: by boat from Portrush.

This is a group of some half dozen islets forming a natural breakwater for Portrush Harbour, and lying in a straight line from W. to E. The principal islets are Castle Island and Long Island.

Popular for bathing, fishing, and picnic parties, the islands offer a pleasant day's excursion. There is a well of drinkable water on one island, and legend tells (though there is no proof) that a Scottish pirate of disrepute, one Tavish Dhu, was buried here.

The Skerry Islands are also said to be the last nesting-place in Ireland of the great auk.

SPANISH ISLES: *see under* Roaringwater Bay Isles.

SPIKE ISLAND

SITUATION: in Cork Harbour, 1 mile S. of Queenstown.
AREA: 45 acres.
POPULATION: 617.
ACCESS: by permission of Irish Military Command for
the area.

Spike Island is today used as an Irish Army coastal
defence station. Ironically, in the days of the British
occupation of Ireland it was the chief prison for leading
Irish rebel patriots. One of its rebel inhabitants in
those days was John Mitchell of Newry, whose *Jail
Journal* was based on his experiences there prior to
his transportation to Botany Bay.

STRANGFORD LOUGH ISLANDS

SITUATION: in Strangford Lough, County Down.
TOTAL AREA: about 450 acres.
ACCESS: by boat from various points in Strangford
Lough, with special permission.

Strangford Lough provides a veritable treat for the
island-lover, for in this long, broad lough which
reaches the sea through a narrow channel just beyond
Portaferry, he will find some thirty-nine islands (many
of them hardly more than rocks) of every shape, size,

K

Strangford Lough Islands (National Trust)

and variety, set in some of the most beautiful scenery in Northern Ireland.

The principal attraction of these islands is that they form part of an ambitious and unusually interesting Wildlife Scheme, which covers about 80 per cent of the foreshore of the Lough as well as the islands themselves. The National Trust controls a good deal of this area.

One of the objects of the Wildlife Scheme is to provide an opportunity for the public to enjoy the wildlife of the Lough. Two viewpoints have been established, at Reagh Island and North East Refuge, where birds can be seen nesting and feeding. Facilities are provided for schools and other groups to use the islands as an outdoor classroom, and a Field Education Officer is available to give advice and information. Volunteer groups from clubs affiliated to the Joint Council of Wildfowling Clubs and ornithologists work under the supervision of the Chief Warden on predator control, eliminating rats and hooded crows. The Trust also carries out a programme for the improvement of wildlife habitat, notably controlling the growth of the spartina plant.

Bird refuges have been set up on several islands, and wildfowling is permitted in certain areas, particularly on Trainor and Shoan Islands. Some 130 species of bird have been recorded in the Lough, the most important of these being geese – brent, greylag, Canada, and barnacle; isolated appearances of both bean and pinkfoot geese have also been recorded. Up to 250 large swans gather each winter in the NE. corner of the Lough.

Wigeon, teal, golden-eye, pintail, tufted duck, and the red-breasted merganser are to be found, and mallard and shelduck breed on the islands in summer. Tern arrive about the end of March: first the sandwich tern and later the arctic and roseate varieties, breeding chiefly on the islands on the w. side, particularly on the Sheelahs, Gabbot, and the Bortrees. On some of the larger islands heron, hooded crow, rooks, linnets, willow warblers, and robins can be seen.

Smaller birds on these islands include knot, dunlin, redshank, oyster-catcher, and bar-tailed godwit, with occasional visits from curlew, sandpiper, whimbrel, and such predators as the buzzard, peregrine, sparrow hawk, and short-eared owl.

Seals inhabit the smaller islands, the majority of the pups being born late in June. One of the most colourful spectacles is the pageantry provided on some of the islands in summer by a wide range of butterflies, including the common blue, said in this area to be the largest and most brilliant in Europe, the tortoise-shell, peacock, brown, and white; while many reports have been made of uncommon and noteworthy moths.

The marine and plant life of the islands is extremely varied, 1,200 different species of marine animal having been recorded. Fish in the Lough include haddock, sea trout, dogfish, tope, sole, plaice, blennies, gobies, pipe fish, sucker fish, and sand eels. Sea urchins, sun stars, sea hares, and the curled octopus are common below low water mark. The suitability of the area for marine research led to the establishment of the Queen's University (Belfast) Marine Biological Station at Portaferry in 1945.

Mahee (q.v.) and Reagh are the two largest islands; most of the others are very small. Causeways link some of the islands to the mainland. Centuries ago the islands were settled by both Celtic monks and Norse seamen. Today several of the islands are leased by the Trust from private owners, including the winter refuge islands of the Bortrees, Sheelah's, Peggy's, Jane's Rock (all leased from Mr W. Montgomery, of Rosemount, Greyabbey, Newtownards, Co. Down), Jackdaw Island (owned by dependants of the late Cdr King Hall), and Pig Island (leased from the Lady Mairi Bury, Mount Stewart, Newtownards). The following islands have predator control agreements: Dunsey Rock, Inisharoan, Parton Inishanier, Round Island, Long Island, Hen Island, and Lythe Rock.

Shooting: this is allowed on a permit, obtainable from the National Trust, 82 Dublin Road, Belfast, BT2 7JA.

Seasonal permits are available to members of clubs affiliated to The Joint Council of Wildfowling, £1. Seasonal permits to other individuals, £8. Day permits £1·50. Permits do not entitle holders to shoot above Mean High Tide mark.

Book: *Strangford Lough*, published by the National Trust Committee for Northern Ireland, 1971.

TAWIN

SITUATION: 1 mile NNW. of Kilcolgan Point on S. side of the approach to Galway Harbour, County Galway.
AREA: approximately 300 acres.
POPULATION: uninhabited.
ACCESS: by boat from Galway.

Tawin is much smaller than it appears at low water, for the island consists mainly of sand shoals which extend for about 2 miles. A pleasant place for picnicking and bathing in summer.

TEARAGHT

SITUATION: one of the Blaskets group, 8 miles WSW. of Slea Head, County Kerry.
AREA: 40 acres.
POPULATION: uninhabited.
ACCESS: by boat from Dunquin.

The most westerly of the Blaskets (q.v.), Tearaght is also the least accessible of them. It is reputed to be the island from which St Brandon set off in quest of the 'Blessed Isles of the West'.

TORY

SITUATION: 8 miles N. of the NW. corner of County Donegal.
AREA: 4 miles long and 1 mile wide.
POPULATION: 250 (1966).
ACCESS: by boat from the mainland. Services depend on the tide. The mailboat operates on Mondays, Wednesdays, and Fridays, leaving Magheroarty Pier at 10.00 a.m. Some private services also run. Helicopter trips depart from Rosapena Hotel.

Not an easy island to reach except in good weather, Tory is desolate and treeless, and yet still fascinating. It is composed mainly of rocks, with a very thin covering of soil, and even this has been eroded by the inhabitants cutting away peat for fuel.

There are high cliffs at the NW. end of Tory and it has always been a graveyard for shipping; evidence of this is provided by the iron plates from wrecked ships which are often to be seen doing duty as grates in island homes. Agriculture is carried on with the most primitive of implements, including ploughs and harrows made from iron bolts from wrecked ships.

It is said that the inhabitants of Tory live to a great age. Certainly they have had their share of centenarians. Perhaps because of this the history of Tory is a strange

Tory Island, County Donegal (Irish Tourist Board)

mixture of legend and fact, the chief figure in the mythology being Balor, the god-chief of the Formorians, a race of pirates who once occupied the island. The story of Balor is part and parcel of Celtic mythology.

Balor was known as the God of Darkness, or Balor of the Baleful eye, and he is represented with one eye in his forehead. He was, however, slain by his son-in-law Hugh, God of Light. Two rocks on the E. side of the island are regarded as Balor's castle and prison.

The name Tory means 'towered', and possibly this

originated from the round bell tower in the west village, built in the era of Viking domination. Constructed of rounded beach stones, it was originally 57 ft high. It is probable that a prehistoric fort existed here, as some earthworks are still visible. St Columcille is said to have founded a monastery on the island in the 6th century. There are ruins of two churches, and a 7ft undecorated mica-slate cross. Some 'cursing stones', alleged to have been effectively used on 22 September 1884, are regarded with affection locally. On that date the gunboat *Wasp* tried to land police and soldiers on Tory to collect taxes, only to have their craft destroyed with great loss of life. Coincidentally, one reward of living on the island today is that there are no taxes, rates, or rents.

Nor for that matter are there any rats. A curious legend of Tory is that rats cannot live there, being allergic to what is called Tory clay. Some islanders will give specimens of local clay to those genuinely seeking to keep rats away.

One of the more sinister places on the island is St Columcille's Hole, reputed to be the place where the javelin landed when St Columcille hurled it to seek a site to found a church. It is 70 ft deep by about 150 ft wide at the top and, writes Kevin Crossley-Holland, 'is a precipitous tumble of red rock, an improbable and frightening pit. In one corner there is a passage out to the sea. You can see the water far below, dark and gleaming, ramming and sucking in the passage . . . the last generation would not go near Columcille's Hole in the dark for fear of the *sheegees*, the fairies.'

In 1832 Lloyds had their signal station on Tory. Now a modern lighthouse maintains a watch on the seas. Most of the people are engaged in lobster fishing and small mixed farming. There are two main villages, East and West, the latter having electricity. There are two shops, one of which is a combination of shop, pub, and post office, and also possesses the island's only telephone.

Tory is not without a few pretensions to culture. The pub-keeper plays the tin whistle, pipes, and accordion, and encourages musical evenings, while a few years ago a visiting English painter discovered some latent talent on the island. He encouraged the efforts of four local artists, and finally arranged exhibitions of their work. One of the paintings was bought by the Northern Ireland Arts Council.

An interesting feature of the island is the Tory canoe, which bears a close resemblance to the early currachs. It is made of sally rods fastened together by strands of twisted horse-hair, though modified today in many respects.

Accommodation: there is limited accommodation provided by cottagers.

Books: *Problems of Smaller Territories*, edited by B. Benedict, Athlone Press, 1967, contains an article by J. R. Fox on Tory Island; *The Islands of Ireland*, by Thomas H. Mason, Mercier Press, Cork, rev. edn. 1967; *Pieces of Land: Journeys to Eight Islands*, by Kevin Crossley-Holland, Gollancz, 1972.

TRAINOR ISLAND: *see under* Strangford Lough Islands.

VALENTIA

SITUATION: less than ½ mile off the Iveragh Peninsula, County Kerry, and 3 miles W. of Cahirciveen.
AREA: 10 sq. miles.
POPULATION: 1,625.
ACCESS: by ferry from Reenard to Knightstown.

There has been some colourful disputation as to the origin of the name of this island. Some romantically still insist it got its name from Valencia in Spain, and was given it by survivors from a wrecked vessel of the Armada who landed here. The truth is, however, that Valentia is a corruption of Bheil Inse, meaning 'island by the river mouth'.

It is a lovely island with a soft, mild climate, especially in winter, and myrtle, arbutus, fuschias, tree ferns, magnolias, and many sub-tropical plants bloom here. The harbour is deep and sheltered, with a narrow entrance, and perhaps because of this was in the past the haunt of smugglers and pirates. The shores are indented with cliffs and tiny bays, and to some extent sheltered in places by isolated rocks. Bray Head, Valentia's most western point, rises to 792 ft, and its summit provides magnificent views across to the Skelligs, the Blaskets, and the Dingle Mountains.

The best cliff scenery on the island is in the N. in the area known as Fogher Cliffs, but the flower-covered interior is the most attractive part of Valentia. For many years it was only occasionally visited by outsiders, but since World War II tourism has been introduced and visitors are catered for. The principal

Valentia Island, County Kerry (Irish Tourist Board)

town, Knightstown, gets its name from the Knights of Kerry, to whom Valentia originally belonged. An Irish cross to the memory of one of the Knights of Kerry stands on high ground near the entrance to the harbour. Nearby is a lighthouse, the beams of which are visible at a distance of 10 miles. The lighthouse stands on a headland known as Cromwell's Fort, so called because the Lord Protector once built forts at each end of the island.

Most of the inhabitants live by farming and fishing, but tourism is becoming increasingly important as a means of making a living here. There are facilities for golf, boating, sea-fishing, and bathing. The road from

Knightstown runs right across the island, which is waisted and low in the middle, and rises again towards the wireless station near Bray Head. *En route* the road passes some disused slate quarries from which a footpath leads to the cliffs.

Valentia was the eastern terminal of the first trans-atlantic cable. After several abortive attempts, a cable was first laid in 1858 to Trinity Bay in Newfoundland. Today there are several cables leading from the cable station at Knightstown.

See also Beginish, Church Island (Kerry).

Accommodation: there is a 32-room hotel at Knights-town, and other accommodation on the island, but demand almost always exceeds supply in the summer.

Post Office and banks.

Places of interest: Glanleam, a private estate formerly belonging to the Knights of Kerry, is worth visiting for its beautiful grounds and flowers.

WEST CALF: *see under* Roaringwater Bay Isles.

WEST DUNKERRON: *see under* Greenan and The Dunkerrons.

WESTPORT BAY ISLANDS

SITUATION: in the innermost part of Westport Bay, close to Westport, County Mayo.
TOTAL AREA: 300 acres.

POPULATION: partially inhabited.
ACCESS: by boat from Westport.

There are several of these islets dotted around West-port Bay, some close together, giving the impression from afar of yellow-tinted baby ducks clustering together in the water. They are mainly isles of yellow clay, embedded with lime and sandstone.

Ranging from 90 ft to 110 ft high, most of the islands have cliffs on their N. and W. sides. Dorinish (q.v.) is near the S. shore of the mainland and about 8 cables S. of Inishgort lighthouse: this is one of the few islands which are inhabited. Others are Moynish More, $7\frac{1}{2}$ miles ENE. of Achillbeg; Roeillaun, $\frac{3}{4}$ mile SE. of Moynish, lying near the N. shore about 6 miles N. of Teckanvy Point; Inishoo, the island with the highest ground, $2\frac{1}{2}$ miles SE. of Moynish More; and Inishgort, $\frac{3}{4}$ mile S. of Inishoo, which has a lighthouse 92 ft high.

WEST SKEAM: *see under* Roaringwater Bay Isles.

WHIDDY

SITUATION: close inshore to Bantry at the NE. tip of Bantry Bay.
AREA: 2 sq. miles.
POPULATION: 60 (1966).
ACCESS: by boat from Bantry ($1\frac{3}{4}$ miles), by private arrangement only with local fishermen. Advance notice is necessary: contact the Irish Tourist Office, The Square, Bantry.

This long, low-lying island, with its macadamised surfaces, is no beauty spot. Its chief significance today is as a terminal for oil tankers. In 1969 the Gulf Oil Corporation established an oil distribution installation on the island, and some of the largest tankers in the world ply between Kuwait and the oil terminal on Whiddy.

Most of the inhabitants, however, are engaged in farming, which they carry on undisturbed by the huge terminal at the w. end of the island. Whiddy is said to have some of the richest grazing land in County Cork: its name means 'fat, good grass'.

The remains of an old castle built by O'Sullivan Bere in the reign of Henry VI survive. It was here that in 1789 the French tried to land troops to launch a rebellion in Ireland against the British. From that date until Ireland achieved independence Whiddy was used as a Royal Naval base; traces of this can still be seen.

WHITE ISLAND: *see under* Garvan Isles.

YELLOW: *see under* Blaskets, The.